HARLEY-DAVIDSON

MOTORCYCLES FROM MILWAUKEE

Abbeydale Press

HARLEY-DAVIDSON

MOTORCYCLES FROM MILWAUKEE

MIRCO DE CET

This edition printed in 2008.

First published by Abbeydale Press.
An imprint of Bookmart Limited.

Trading as Bookmart Limited
Blaby Road, Wigston
Leicestershire LE18 4SE
England

© 2007 Bookmart Limited

ISBN: 978-1-86147-207-6

10 9 8 7 6 5 4 3 2

Produced for Bookmart Limited by:
Editorial Developments,
Edgmond, Shropshire,
England

Design by: Bacroom Design and Advertising,
Birmingham, England

Index: Marie Lorimer Indexing Services, Harrogate,
England

Registered Number 2372865

Printed in Thailand

Forward

Harley-Davidson. No other manufacturer's name in recent history is globally known as well as is this name. This name and trademark 'Bar and Shield' represent several things... freedom, rebellion, lifestyle, individualism and, last but not least, a motorcycle.

Through my experiences I have discovered that the Harley-Davidson story is one of commitment to people. The early days, when William Harley and brothers Walter and Arthur Davidson worked to develop a motor driven cycle in a wooden shed located in Milwaukee, were committed to moving people with a form of transportation that was affordable. The war years provided a testing ground to better understand the mobility needs of a country and how diverse a motorcycle could be to meet these needs. The post war years found servicemen returning from all over the world with a new outlook on life. A lot of these people wanted to experience the freedom they had fought for. This was a time of discovery in an economically strong country and a lot of people found this freedom on a motorcycle, a Harley-Davidson motorcycle. The same motorcycle that proved itself time and time again during the war.

The post war clubs and activities surrounding motorcycles found participation with machines from all manufacturers of the time. The Harley-Davidson name emerged as the motorcycle of choice and developed a loyal and well organised following. A motorcycle lifestyle for people emerged. The Company responded by supporting this lifestyle with accessories and apparel to create individual identities for the motorcycle and its owner.

Racing has long been a source of entertainment and product development. Harley-Davidson has recognised this from the beginning and established itself in this area as well. From the 'Board Track' years of the teens to the drag strips of today, the Harley-Davidson motorcycle has proven its worth.

Today we see the 'hard core' biker and envy the freedom. These guys exist today as a testament to the birth of the 'freedom movement' and the rebellion found with motorcycles. But sometimes a closer look at these men, and yes women, you will find these riders are simply people, like you, that have found the secret to enjoying the simple things in life, being themselves in a brotherhood of individuals, on a Harley-Davidson.

Jeff Ray
Executive Director
Barber Vintage Motorsports Museum
Birmingham, Alabama USA

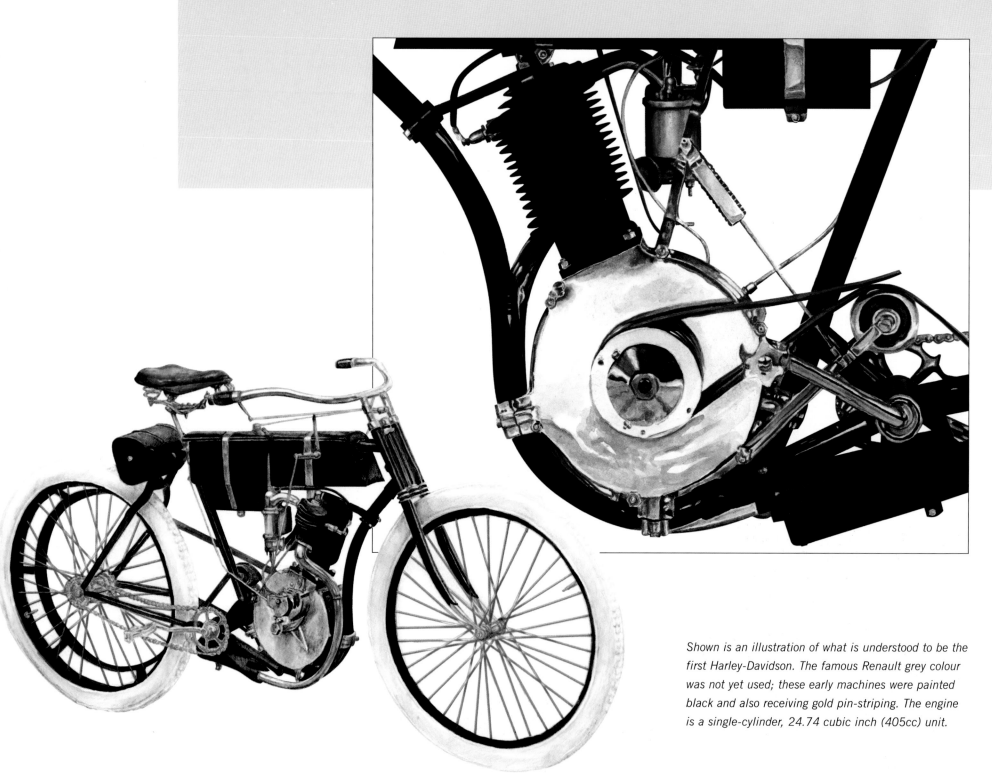

Shown is an illustration of what is understood to be the first Harley-Davidson. The famous Renault grey colour was not yet used; these early machines were painted black and also receiving gold pin-striping. The engine is a single-cylinder, 24.74 cubic inch (405cc) unit.

1903 The First Production Harley-Davidson

The Early Years

The town of Littleport is located in the mid-eastern part of England, twenty miles north of the university city of Cambridge. It was here that William Harley was born in Victoria Street, in 1835. Harley emigrated to Oswego in the United States in 1859, and even fought in the American Civil War. After the conflict, William and his then wife, Mary Smith, gave birth to several children, of which one was named William Sylvester Harley, who was born on December 29, 1880, in Milwaukee. It would also be here in Milwaukee, that the now legendary motorcycle company would also see birth. Arthur Davidson,

born in 1881 and the youngest of three brothers, would join up with his old school-friend, William S. Harley, to found the Harley-Davidson motorcycle company in 1903.

Two years prior to this, and at the tender age of twenty-one, William Harley had produced a blueprint drawing of a single-cylinder engine, which could be fitted to a standard pushbike. It would be a similar configuration that would be presented as the first Harley-Davidson motorcycle in 1903, following several prototypes – if they could be called that.

Both William and Arthur were technically minded, and once the machines proved themselves to be reliable, or at least able to run consistently without breaking down too often – they were joined by Arthur's brother Walter. Walter had the mechanical expertise to help in the construction of what was to become the first Harley-Davidson machine, and so it was that he joined his brother and friend on a full-time basis, thus making the third founding member. During this time, William, the oldest of the Davidson brothers and the last of the founding members to join the company, was involved with the company too but only on a part-time basis.

The first machine the foursome produced used a single-cylinder engine, and was fitted to a modified bicycle frame, with final drive being by leather belt. The power produced by the little engine was enough to propel it along a level street, but inclines were a difficulty, and generally required the rider to pedal at the same time to give added momentum. The machine wasn't the familiar grey of the models that followed, but black with gold pinstriping.

This photograph, taken around 1915, shows the four founders of the Company - L to R: Arthur Davidson, Walter Davidson, William S. Harley and William A Davidson.

The memorial dedicated to William Harley, father of William Sylvester Harley. This can be found in the town of Littleport, England.

The original workshop where it all started. It was in here over one hundred years ago that the first machines were assembled.

And so the Harley-Davidson Company was formed, the words handwritten on the door of their first workshop – a fifteen foot by ten foot shed, located in the Davidson family backyard.

Just a year later in 1904, C H Lang, a Chicago businessman, set up the first dealership, and sold one of the first three production Harley-Davidson motorcycles ever made by the fledgling company. By 1905 considerably more machines had been manufactured and the company took on its first full-time employee. With business turnover increasing, a move to newer and bigger premises was necessary and happened in 1906. A new building measuring twenty-eight feet by eighty feet was acquired in what was then Chestnut Street (today known as Juneau Avenue) and staff numbers were increased to six, to cope with the steady flow of new orders. During 1906, a new colour scheme was also introduced on some machines. Renault grey with red pinstriping was to be the new colour, and contributed to the machines becoming known as 'Silent Grey Fellow' – this being a description given to the bikes because of their new Renault grey paintwork, and the fact that they ran so quietly. Production figures increased rapidly through the next few years, and where 1905 saw some sixteen machines built, by 1908 some 450 machines were rolling out of the new premises.

Silent grey fellow

Model	1910 Model 6
Engine	Air Cooled, Single Cylinder, Four-Stroke
Ignition	Battery
Displacement	30cu.in / 500cc
Fuel System	Single Schebler Carburettor
Transmission	Single speed
Suspension	Duel spring fork
Brakes	Rear coaster
Weight	225 lbs
Top Speed	45 mph

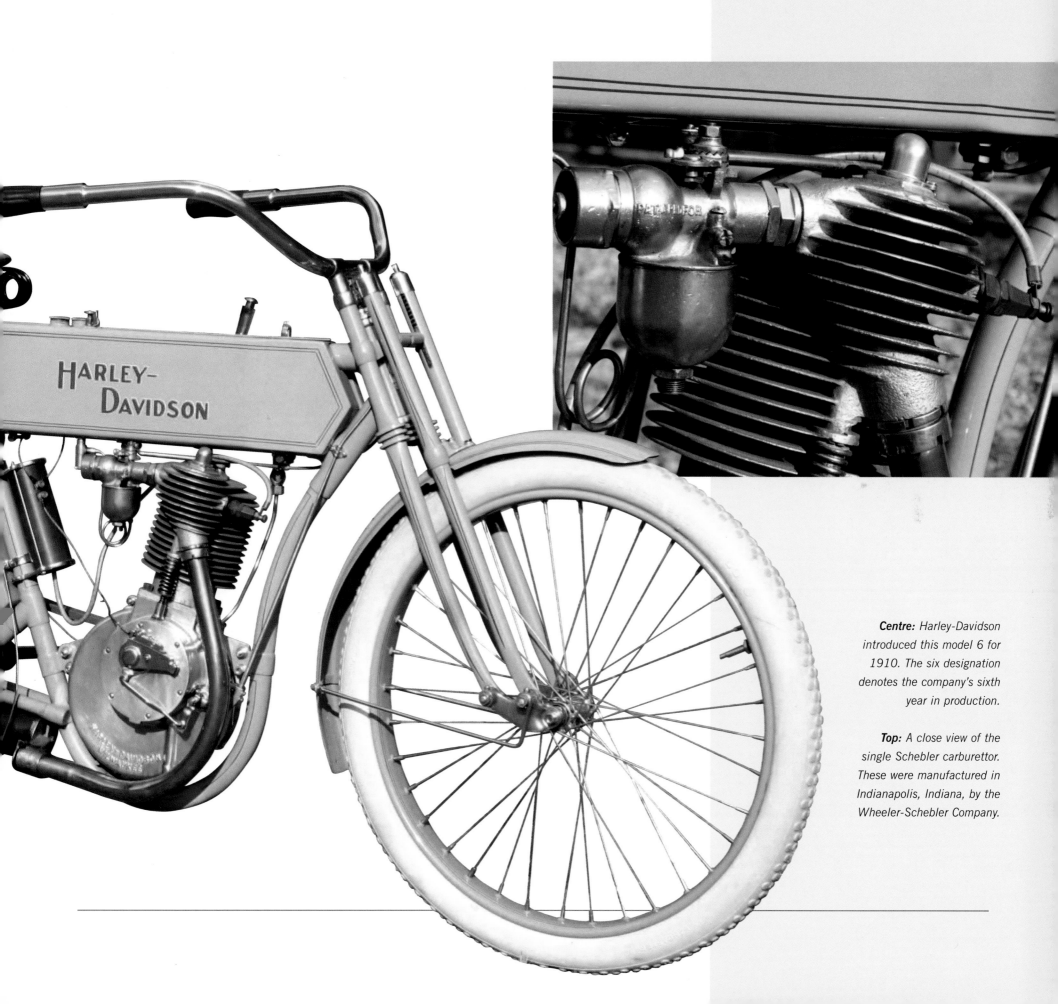

HARLEY-DAVIDSON

Centre: Harley-Davidson introduced this model 6 for 1910. The six designation denotes the company's sixth year in production.

Top: A close view of the single Schebler carburettor. These were manufactured in Indianapolis, Indiana, by the Wheeler-Schebler Company.

Left: The slack drive belt is due to the control lever being in the incorrect position. Once pulled backwards, it would tighten the belt ready for action.

Below: The configuration of the engine and its components are viewed easily here.

1910 Model 6

A stunning looking machine; now housed at the Wheels Through Time museum in Maggie Valley, NC, USA.

The year 1907 was a significant one for the company. William Davidson quit his job with the Milwaukee Road railroad, to join the company on a full-time basis, and therefore completing the formation of the founding members. In September of this year the company was also officially incorporated, with shares being split four ways and distributed to the four founders. Production continued to increase

and more staff and workspace was also provided. Harley-Davidson was now truly on its way to becoming a major motorcycle producer. Over the next year, Walter continued to show how reliable and tough their machines were with his endurance outings, and in 1908 finished the seventh annual Federation of American Motorcyclists endurance and reliability contest with a perfect score. He

This is a fine example of an X8 model of 1912. Seen in the centre of the rear wheel is the housing for the 'free wheel control'.

1912 X8

This is the 30 cubic inch, IOE, F-head engine of the 1912 X8, which gave the machine a top speed of around 50 mph (80 kph).

also achieved a staggering 188.234 miles per gallon economy record, just three days later. With these kinds of results, let alone those that were not reported, the Harley-Davidson name and reputation for reliability was starting to spread far and wide, and very quickly.

Police departments across America have always been associated with Harley-Davidson machines, and in 1908 the very first machines were delivered to the Detroit, Michigan, police department. The company built up a good relationship with many police departments around the United States and continues to deliver machines to them, right up to the present day.

Suspension for the rider was improved considerably this year. The already rear-sprung saddle was also fitted with a spring within the down tube.

Left: *No mistaking which make of machine this is, the company badge clearly seen between the duel sprung forks.*

Top Right: *The belt final drive can clearly be seen, and the handle used to adjust it stretches up from it.*

Bottom Right: *The machine still used pedal power to start. Once started it would be taken off the stand and away it would go.*

Although progress had been made with these early machines, it was clear that the team could not rest on its laurels. William Harley had been working hard on a new design, which would have a bigger engine and more power. This machine was presented in 1909 and became the company's first V-twin, a configuration that was to become synonymous with the name Harley-Davidson, and which is still used to this day.

The model 5D, as it became known, performed well at its first official endurance outing, scoring the maximum points, which must have given its rider, Walter Davidson, great satisfaction. Unfortunately the machine wasn't quite as reliable as it seemed, with the new V-twin engines being plagued by valve-gear problems. A new and improved version was presented in 1911 as the 7D, which was fitted

The 1913 Harley-Davidson series 9, was generally known as the 5-35, because it produced 5hp from its 35 cubic inch engine.

The X8 is seen next to an unrestored 1913 model 9B. Many collectors like to keep their exhibits in this way as it gives it more authenticity.

1913 9B

with a mechanical inlet valve, and a drive belt tensioner. The new valve control system allowed the machine to perform better, and the tensioner stopped the drive belt from slipping, therefore making the machine much more reliable. Along with other improvements the new twin was transformed into a machine that was up to the usual Harley-Davidson standard.

Although 1911 was a good sales year, there was a cry from dealerships and riders for more power. They had seen their main competitor, Indian, take a 1, 2, 3 win at the Isle of Man TT races, and so wanted much of the same for themselves – chain drive, was the cry, and more horsepower. And so it was that in 1912 Harley-Davidson produced exactly that with their Model 8 machines.

Comfort was enhanced by fitting a spring inside the seat down-tube, along with other frame design changes. The engine was made more powerful, whilst a new clutch system known as 'free wheel control,' a first for Harley, was fitted to the rear wheel, and worked via a lever positioned on the left side of the machine.

Shown here is a Sport Roadster, Model K of 1915; a rare machine to say the least. It is thought to be the only one in existence.

The Sport Roadster has a classic 1000cc pocket valve engine fitted, along with single-speed transmission. Top speed is around 90 mph.

The rare Cygnet rear car attachment, could carry two passengers, and as a three-wheeler benefited from a lower taxation bracket.

A 1915 Harley-Davidson, with rear buggy. The new three-speed transmission helped with performance, especially in this configuration.

There was also, for the first time, a choice of belt or chain driven machines – 8D, X8D, and X8E respectively. Signs of how well the company was doing were shown when this same year building work started on new premises in Juneau Avenue, Milwaukee, which today is the headquarters and the main factory of the Harley-Davidson Company. A new parts department was also set up and by 1916 the company was producing something in the region of 17,000 single and V-twin machines of varying designations. Amongst the machines now being manufactured, there was the addition of three-speed transmissions, automatic oil pumps, kick starters and full electrical systems, all of which added to the rider's comfort and safety.

1917 model J with sidecar

Although this rare 1917 Harley and side-car are unrestored, they are used practically every day. Keeping them in their original state gives the ensemble a real natural feel for the period.

The 1917 Model J used a 16hp, 61 cubic inch (1000cc) engine with three-speed transmission. It needed plenty of power to pull the side-car and its passenger.

Although slow to fully engage in the sporting scene, Harley-Davidson did venture into the fight in 1913. (See 'The Wrecking Crew.')

During all this activity, a war had broken out in Europe that engulfed most of the world. America found itself sending troops to Europe and other parts of the globe, after war was declared on the Austro-Hungarian Empire and its many allies. Harley-Davidson, along with other motorcycle manufacturers, also became involved, with production now being centred mainly on military requirements.

This was not the first war they had supplied motorcycles for: machines had seen action during the uprising against the infamous Pancho Villa. Fitted with sidecars and machine guns, they were used as border patrol vehicles under General Pershing. During the First World War, the 61 cubic inch model was used as the standard military machine. It was generally fitted with a sidecar and, as mentioned, would often have a machine gun too. A Service School was set up in 1917, initially as a military initiative, but which would later also serve as a civilian department for training in riding instruction, as well as maintenance of the Harley-Davidson machines.

The flat twin configuration was a complete change from the conventional Harley-Davidson. Seen here is the front cylinder.

The flat, twin-cylinder configuration ran back to front, rather than protruding from either sides of the machine.

Known as the Sport Twin, the 1920 model W had a 35 cubic inch (575cc) engine and three-speed transmissions.

The sturdy F-head, 61 cubic inch (1000cc), V-Twin engine of the 1920 Model J.

Seen on top of the fuel tank is the speedometer, and on the left is the gear-change mechanism.

The terminology 'Big Twin' was now being used to distinguish these machines from the Sports models.

Schebler carburettor and three-speed transmission helped to power the model J to a heady 65 mph (105 kph).

The first model J was introduced in 1915 and became a steady seller for the company. This is a 1920 example.

A few days prior to the end of the war, Corporal Roy Holtz was driving his company captain on a reconnaissance mission on his Harley-Davidson, when they ended up in a German field camp and were taken prisoner. Fortunately they were released after the armistice, three days later, which resulted in Roy being the first American serviceman to be on German soil, and with his Harley-Davidson.

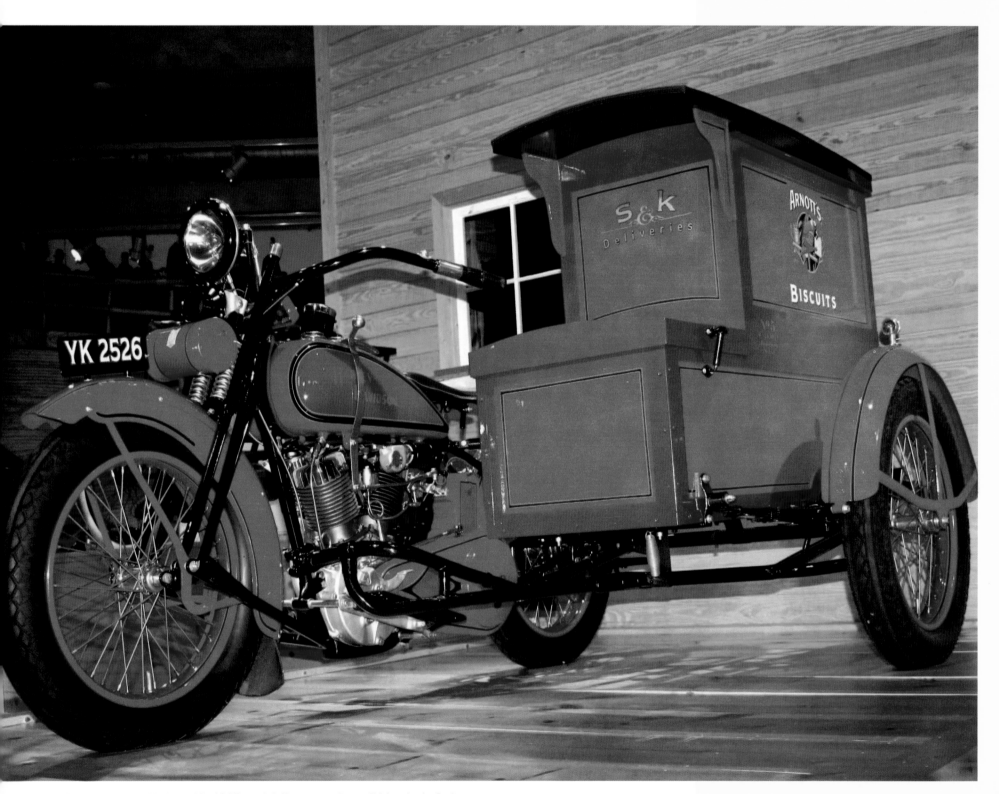

A typical export Harley, this 1925 model JD was used to sell biscuits in Sydney, NSW, Australia.

Post-war, the company produced a machine that was completely out of context, a horizontal twin. It took the title of Sport Twin, but sales weren't great in the home market. Perhaps a little too radical, it didn't catch the imagination in the United States, but fortunately did abroad, where it sold well. The cylinders ran fore and aft, rather than protruding from either side of the machine. The company had now done away with Renault grey paintwork and during the early 1920s machines were painted Brewster green, which was soon displaced by olive green, which was used until the early 1930s. By 1920, Harley-Davidson took the title of the largest motorcycle manufacturer in the world with 2,000 dealers in sixty-seven countries around the world.

Post-war euphoria turned to 1920s depression and sales started to fall. Henry Ford reduced the price of his cars so dramatically that they were on a par to those being asked for motorcycles, and suddenly things didn't look quite so rosy in the motorcycle world. For 1921 the 74 cubic inch was introduced, an upgraded version of the 61 cubic inch V-twin. It was used to combat the ever-growing tide of large four-cylinder machines being produced by the likes of Indian, Henderson, and Cleveland.

The new twins were initially intended for sidecar work, but customers were pleased to be able to have the extra power to compete with the big fours around at the time. The new machines were advertised as 'Superpowered Twins' due to their 18hp output.

The JD engine was an upgraded version of the J, becoming a 74 cubic inch (1207cc), 18 hp unit.

The venerable Harley 45, which was produced between 1929 and 1973, became the most versatile of engines produced by the company. It became an alternative to the Big Twin machines, used during the Second World War, fitted to the Servi-car and also competed in dirt track racing across America, winning numerous trophies. This is a 1947, 750cc version.

1958 Rikuo

The Rikuo was the result of a deal done with the Sankyo Seiyako Corp., of Japan back in the 1930s.

Although Harley-Davidson were the best-selling machines, they still felt a need to counteract the models that Indian were bringing out, and when Indian introduced their single-cylinder Prince, Harley-Davidson responded by introducing their first singles for three years – the A, AA, B, and BA models. These were all 350cc, with the AA, an overhead-valve model, built primarily for racing and presented at a 1925 race in Milwaukee. This particular machine soon acquired the nickname of 'Peashooter,' which was due to the rather raspy exhaust note it created. Although the model A, which was fitted with a magneto, and model B, fitted with a battery, used a side-valve engine the BA was an overhead-valve model. These two side-valve machines sold well in Europe and Australia, where mid-range single-cylinder machines were well received.

From 1925 Harley-Davidson changed the shape of their fuel tanks and they now came in a teardrop shape, which all machines soon inherited. For 1928 a new Two Cam engine was presented, which came in two versions – the JH, a 61 cubic inch, 1000cc machine, and the JDH, a larger 74 cubic inch, 1200cc machine. The engine had its roots in the Harley-Davidson racing department, and inherited many of the racing refinements of the period, allowing the larger machine to reach some 100mph. The end of the 1920s saw the introduction of

The Servi-car, introduced in 1932, served the company well for over forty years. It used the forty-five, (750cc), V-Twin, flathead engine.

the model D, a V-twin, 750cc machine, and the model C, a single-cylinder 500cc machine. It would take some time before the model D, or Forty-five as it was known, would reach its full potential, whilst production of the model C was stopped in 1934.

What followed was the V and VL, which again were no great shakes, being plagued with mechanical problems. It was, though, the steady improvement and final reliability of the model D and the V that saw Harley-Davidson through the extremely difficult early 1930s.

The Wall Street crash of 1929 saw businesses going to the wall by the thousands, people were jumping from the tops of skyscrapers, and business dipped to an all-time low. Harley-Davidson production hit the skids, and where they were selling some 17,000 machines in 1930, only about 3,700 were sold in 1933. The panic was for real, and it was felt through every industry in the USA. During this time Harley-Davidson cut back on everything it could, including workers' wages, and the workforce itself.

Exports were also being hit hard, and it is interesting to note that prior to the Great Depression, one area of sales that was doing very well was Japan. But with the now unfavourable exchange rate they were starting to plummet, to say the least. It was an independent business agent by the name of Alfred Rich Child, who had the idea that if the Japanese were sold the tooling for the machines, they could manufacture the motorcycles in their own country at a considerably lower price, and therefore sales would once again be buoyant.

This is the model VL of 1931. It had a 74 cubic inch (1208cc) engine and produced some 30hp.

Right: *There was little money for new ideas in the 1930s and so looks were all important. Smart colour schemes started to appear.*

Centre: *The forty-fives, re-designated the R series, were given an upgrade, which included new cylinders for better heat dispersal.*

Model	1933 Model RL
Engine	Flathead, Side valve, V-Twin
Power Rating	18.5 hp
Ignition	Battery
Displacement	45.32cu.in /746.33cc
Fuel System	Schebler Deluxe Carburettor
Transmission	Three-speed
Suspension	Front: Leading link spring fork
Brakes	Front: drum
	Rear: contracting band
Weight	475 lbs
Top Speed	84 mph

And so it was that Harley-Davidson, in agreement with the Home Office, decided to allow machine tools and licenses to be sold to the Japanese Sankyo Seiyako Corporation, who proceeded to build and sell the Harley-Davidson machines. These machines, although direct copies of the Harley-Davidson model, now used the Rikuo name on the tank – strangely enough the name translates into 'Land King' or 'King of Road.' The company continued to sell the machines for many years to come, even using them in military form during the Second World War.

1933 RL HARLEY-DAVIDSON

With the Great Depression hitting hard, much emphasis was put on attractive looks - note the stylised new logo on this tank.

Note the toolbox, fitted neatly under the front light. This would be repositioned in 1934 to behind the gearbox.

The model VLD Special Sport solo was introduced in 1933. there were 29 variations of the 'V' series built between 1920 and 1936.

By 1931 the only competitor left was their old rival Indian; the rest had fallen by the wayside during the sales slump. Indian too were struggling though, and after being taken over by the Du Pont company, started a rationalisation program, which left Harley-Davidson in a slightly stronger position than before. Even so, Indian were still presenting new ideas and even bigger machines. Harley-Davidson responded with the VLH, a machine that was fitted with the biggest engine yet produced. There was also a colours war on, with machines being painted in all sorts of attractive colour schemes. The drab olive green was relegated and bright new oranges, creams, and reds came in, along with an Art Deco, eagle-design tank logo. Machines were upgraded and modified to make them more appealing; chroming was a new feature as were fishtail exhaust pipes. The Forty-five was also upgraded and redesignated the R series, whilst the little thirty-fifty machines were also treated to similar upgrades. All these small but significant changes, along with new sales and marketing ideas, helped to see the company through the most dreadful period of stagnant sales.

Headlight, toolbox and leading link forks, made up the front end of the VLD.

To rejuvenate their products during a stagnant 1930s, Harley introduced a top of the range, 74 cubic inch model, in a variety of no-extra-cost colours.

Chrome and bright colour schemes were used to attract the dwindling sales during the Great Depression.

The Knucklehead

On many occasions, during a period of instability, companies have had the ability to progress and prepare for the future, and this is what happened at Harley-Davidson. A new design was being worked on, which was due for presentation in 1935, but which unfortunately had to be delayed through no fault of the company. When the Depression started to ease, the new machine made its appearance. The new model E – or as so many now know it, the Knucklehead – was presented in 1936.

The Sixty-one, OHV engine, that we all love and know as the Knucklehead. The nickname derives from the bulging rocker boxes.

Still in original paint, this is a 1936 Knucklehead. It was originally due for presentation in 1935.

It was given this name due to the bulbous rocker boxes fitted to the new overhead-valve engine. With its 61 cubic inch engine, increased power output and exciting styling, the machine became an instant success, everything that a Harley-Davidson rider could want. The Knucklehead immediately took its place in the record books when race rider of the day, Joe Petrali, set a new top speed record of 136mph (219 kph) at Daytona Beach. The success of the new machine suddenly turned the corner for the Harley-Davidson company, and by 1937 sales had climbed again to 11,000. Whilst the Knucklehead took the limelight, other models were quietly being looked at too, with important improvements being incorporated into them also.

Bottom Left: *The Knucklehead engine was the first overhead valve engine made by Harley-Davidson, and it came in 60 and 74 cubic inch sizes. The 74 cubic inch came out in 1941 and produced 40 and 45 horsepower.*

Bottom Right: *Sitting pretty with its Art Deco paintwork, and new leather bags, is this beautifully restored 1938 EL Knucklehead.*

The four-speed gear selector numbers, of the knucklehead, can be clearly identified on the cut-out housing for the lever.

The 120 mph (193 kph) speedometer was introduced in 1937. Immediately prior to this was a 100 mph (161 kph) model with gauges.

Besides looking good, the Knucklehead also had a constant mesh four-speed gearbox assisting the 61 cubic inch (988cc) engine.

Fully-fuelled, the knucklehead weighed some six-hundred pounds, but this didn't stop it from touching the ton (100mph/161 kph).

The Buddy seat looks great and it is well sprung, but the rear suspension was still as rigid as ever.

Many people would say that the Knucklehead was the best looking Harley-Davidson, period. It's easy to understand why.

1940 61 cubic inch model

Front and rear mudguard no longer had painted stripes, this was replaced with steel strips, as seen on this 1940 example.

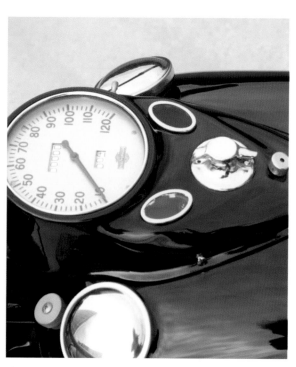

By 1939 all the big twin Harleys had been fitted with upper and lower, self-aligning steering head bearings.

The Airflow rear light was replaced with a larger type, which also had the license plate fitting fitted above it.

No longer was the 120 mph (193kph) speedometer accompanied by dials, just a couple of coloured warning lamps.

Improvements continued to happen for the Knucklehead. Valve train assemblies were enclosed in 1938 and a year later came splined pinion and oil pump drive gears.

Knucklehead also benefited from new valve springs, pistons, intake manifold and transmission in 1939.

Both these machines are of the same year, 1936. Yet they are two different models. In front is a model VX side valve and behind is an EL, OHV model.

Model	1936 Knucklehead EL
Engine	OHV, V-Twin
Power Rating	40 hp
Ignition	Battery
Displacement	60.33cu.in / 988.56cc
Fuel System	1.25in (32mm) Linkert Carburettor
Transmission	Four-speed
Suspension	Front: Spring fork
Brakes	Front/Rear: Drum
Weight	575 lbs
Top Speed	95 mph (153kph)

1936 Knucklehead EL

One machine that wasn't making a stir, but which would be as faithful to the company as a dog is to his master, was the Servi-car, initially dubbed the 'Cycle Tow.' This was a cut-down motorcycle front-end, fitted to a boxed rear-end, with wheels either side. Final drive was via a chain to a car rear axle. Initially launched in 1932, the advertising stated that it was for use by garages, for towing broken-down cars back to the repair stations. Nice idea but unfortunately this didn't work too well. As the machine progressed and became a little more sophisticated and adaptable, towing became easier and safer, with many garages also using the rear box area as an advertising board. The machine was also used

Although the same paintwork as its Knucklehead stablemate, this is in fact a model VX, with new 80 cubic inch engine.

A beautifully restored example of a Knucklehead engine, it's easy to see how the nickname came about.

The new 80 cubic inch flathead engine, was presented in 1936, and was endowed with new cylinder heads and larger cooling fins.

by small companies for delivery of goods and for selling ice-cream, but their biggest use was by police departments for emptying parking meters and giving out traffic tickets.

Over the years, the Servi-car was updated regularly and remained on the books for forty-four years from its introduction in 1932. In later years, owners of these machines would often adorn the rear box with customised paint jobs. Some even removed the original rear box section and replaced it with all manner of strange items.

A 1936 EL Knucklehead Custom, expertly built by Dale Walksler of the Wheels Through Time Museum, Maggie Valley, NC, USA. The colours are in fact 1934 vintage, and the official name is Orlando Orange and of course black.

The engine is 1000cc, and it has a four-speed transmission. Brakes are drum, front and rear, and the handlebars are made by Flanders. The nameplates on the tank are prototypes, and made of aluminium.

Not the most comfortable of seats, but decidedly well sprung for those bumpy roads of the period.

This is the first standard equipment Harley speedometer, 1936 was the only year of the 100 mph (161 kph) unit.

Yes a Knucklehead, but by no means a standard machine. The owner has a registration plate with 'BOBBER' scrawled on it, and that is what it is, with snipped-off tail and custom paint.

Although the Second World War was being fought in Europe and many other parts of the world in 1939, the United States was still reluctant to get involved. It wasn't until the Japanese bombed Pearl Harbor in 1941, that they finally joined the British and their allies to combat the German and Japanese threat. At this time, motorcycle production for civilians was mainly suspended and manufacturing was once again centred on military machines. The civilian Service School, a department that trained mechanics on the maintenance of Harley-Davidson machines, was converted back as the military Quartermasters School.

Even though America had not yet joined the war, they were kept abreast of the situation and in 1939 the US Army made plans to develop a rugged new machine, stipulating that it should be based on the BMW style of motorcycle. A tender went out to Indian and Harley-Davidson to produce prototypes that the army could assess. Both companies knew that a contract with the military would only help to increase sales and see them through the war period, so both came up with a completely new

This machine may pretend to be an EL but there is more to it. Basically a 1939 model, it has a 106 cubic inch motor and six gears. Oh yes, and by the way, it goes like stink!

twin-cylinder machine. Harley-Davidson produced the XA, a pretty good copy of the BMW R71 motorcycle, which was similar to the R75 being used by the German army at the time. This had all the requirements that the army had requested, but was rather expensive to produce. The US Army bought 1,000 of these machines for evaluation, but they never saw action. They finally decided that the WLA, also produced by Harley-Davidson and already in service, was a much cheaper option and would probably do everything that the XA could do. The WLA, basically a civilian W series machine modified for the military, became the standard US military motorcycle, being purchased also by the British, Canadians, Australians, and even the Russians and Chinese.

By the end of the conflict in 1945, Harley-Davidson had produced some 90,000 WLA machines for military use. But with the end of the war came unrest, as the War Department cancelled a large batch of machines, due for war duty.

The result of a request by the military for a BMW style machine, produced the model XA from Harley-Davidson.

The XA was well equipped but also very expensive to manufacture. Because of this, it was never manufactured for the war.

Harley-Davidson had pretty well copied the BMW engine of the period, but not the instrumentation.

Equipped to the gunnels, the WLA had ammunition boxes, gun holster and saddle bags. A radio was often fitted to the rear rack.

The faithful old Military model WLA. Used by so many during the Second World War conflict.

A proud trio of military motorcyclists, kitted out with WLA machines, take time out for a photograph. MP on the mudguard stands for Military Police.

An interesting cut-away of the WLA engine, showing its internal elements.

Much had also happened to the Harley and Davidson families during this period, prompting a new generation of family members to take over the reins of the company. William Davidson had passed away just prior to the conflict in 1937, Walter had also passed away in February of 1942 and William Harley just a year later. The surviving member of the founding four, Arthur Davidson, died in a car accident in 1946. William Davidson's son, yet another William, took over the helm of the company, whilst Harley's son looked after the engineering side of things. The family remained in control of the company, but were to face new challenges in a different and difficult post-war world. Although the Indian company was still a competitor to the company, a much bigger threat was looming – the import of British machines from across the water. Post-war civilian production took a while to really get going, whereas the racing side of things started well. In 1947 the company took over the former A O Smith propeller plant on Capitol Drive, Wauwatosa, which was then used as a machine shop. Products from here were shipped to

This example of a WLA model has seen better days. In fact it was shipped from the continent after the war and kept in this original state.

A little rusty in places but it starts every time. This particular engine has seen some action.

The model U was a machine used mainly for shore patrol by the US Navy (hence USN on the tank).

The signs on the mudguard give away where this machine served - at Agana Naval air Station on the Island of Guam.

The 74 cubic inch (1208cc), V-Twin engine of the model U. Note the well enclosed air filter.

Of the 18,000 motorcycles produced by Harley-Davidson for the war effort, only 366 were 74's.

The Model 165 was introduced in 1953 and replaced the smaller 125. More horsepower and better bodywork made it more attractive.

Juneau Avenue, where the final assembly took place. By 1947 production was back in full swing again and the Knucklehead was given new trim and accessories. This would be its last year of production and several cosmetic changes were made. There was a new tank shape and badge, front mudguard light, and a new rear tail-light, which became known as the 'tombstone' design, and incorporated the rear license plate bracket. More interesting for 1948 was the development of a smaller machine, the little 125S. The machine came about from the appropriation of the DKW

The two-stroke, air-cooled, single-cylinder 165. The basic design came from the German DKW RT125.

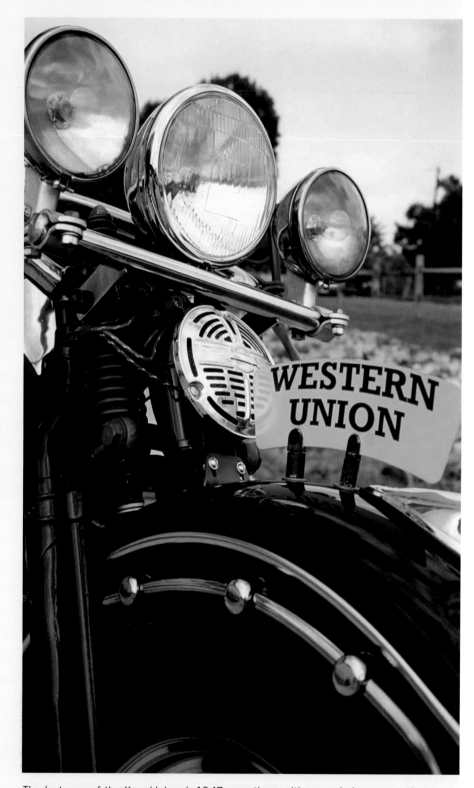

The last year of the Knucklehead, 1947, saw them with several changes, such as stainless steel mudguard trims and a front mudguard lamp.

This particular 1947 FL, was used for delivery duties for the Western Union Telegraph Company, Asheboro, NC, USA.

1947 FL 1200

Tucked neatly under the new shaped tank, is the massive 1200cc engine of the Knucklehead, that soon would be gone forever.

1947 saw Harley-Davidson return to full civilian production and the Knucklehead received several trim and accessory changes.

A new instrument panel was also introduced, with two-tone black and white face, italicised silver numbers and red pointer.

manufacturing rights, after the Second World War. Harley-Davidson and BSA shared these rights and both companies produced their own products derived from the little DKW RT 125 design. The BSA Bantam, one of the best-selling machines ever, was a direct descendant of the acquisition, and although not a great seller, so was the Harley-Davidson 125S. Small-cylinder machines have never really taken off in the United States, and this little 125 was to be no different. Derivatives of the little machine followed – an enlarged 165cc model ST was introduced in 1953, which was uprated in the early 1960s. Even larger 175cc, Ranger, Pacer, and Scat models were offered, and an all-purpose model B, the Hummer, using the basic 125cc engine was introduced in 1955. Even though it wasn't a great seller it did at least introduce a new younger generation of Americans to the motorcycling world, many of whom went on to buy and ride the bigger Harley-Davidson machines – although those who were used to the Big Twins from Milwaukee were a little baffled by the whole idea!

The year 1948 saw the end of the faithful old Knucklehead, which basically acquired a new identity. New features such as aluminium heads, a new hydraulic tappet system, and one-piece, chrome plated, rocker covers, all helped to improve the engine performance, and gave it the new title of 'Panhead' – a reference to the rather saucepan-like rocker covers. The first of the Panhead models looked very similar to the last Knucklehead, but the improvements made all the difference, with the engine running cooler, easier valve adjustment, and the oil being better contained and hitting the right spots. Just a year later, in 1949, the model was fitted with hydraulic front forks, and gained the name Hydra Glide. The forks had been seen briefly on the wartime XA model, and would serve the Big Twins for many years to come.

The new Panhead model was introduced in 1948 and gained its nickname, once again from the shape of its valve covers, which were distinctly Pan shaped. This machine shown is a 1949 example.

1949 Panhead

Model	1949 FL
Engine	OHV, V-Twin
Power Rating	50 hp
Ignition	Battery
Displacement	73.73cu.in /1208.19cc
Fuel System	1.31in (33.3mm) Schebler Carburettor
Transmission	Four-speed
Suspension	Leading link spring/shock fork.
Brakes	Front/Rear: Drum
Weight	565 lbs
Top Speed	100 mph

For 1948 Harley-Davidson introduced Hydra-Glide front forks to the Panhead. This is a later 1957 version.

These 'cheese-grater' style bumpers were very popular in the mid 1950s.

Aluminium heads, hydraulic lifters and saucepan type valve covers, distinguished the Panhead from its predecessor.

The Hydra-Glide name on the forks, denoting that this machine is fitted with this new style of front suspension.

By the beginning of the 1950s, the British in particular, and other European companies had started to export machines to the United States. Slowly at first, but soon in larger numbers. Machines were often being shipped to the United States before being made available in the United Kingdom. America was seen as a lucrative market and the Continental machines were somewhat more advanced than the US-made models, which were still using such controls as the hand gear-change system. Although Harley-Davidson were to see Indian finally throw in the towel, the thought that now there was going to be not just one, but several competitors, must have been like a red rag to a bull. Attempts were made to stop the flow of foreign machines and certainly dealers were encouraged not to work with these foreign invaders. It all came to nothing though and imports came all the same. By 1950, imports accounted for nearly 40 percent of sales in the US and Harley-Davidson were only able to respond with the Model K. Although on paper it seemed to have all the credentials – hand clutch-lever, foot gear-change, and swinging arm rear suspension – it struggled to go over 90mph, had little acceleration and didn't stand a chance against the Triumphs and BSAs of the period, which were already able to reach the magic 'ton' (100 mph).

Here was something quite new, the 1952 750 K Sport, which had suspension at the front and now at the rear too.

1952 750 K sport

As seen here, the 750 K also had foot gearshift, on the right side. A hand operated clutch was also a new addition.

The new style speedometer had large unconventional numbers and a red indicator.

A good looking machine but on the roads of the USA, this machine was being trounced by the imports - British Twins.

This anniversary edition, Hydra-Glide model, of 1954, belonged to the Wilmington Police dpt., NC, USA.

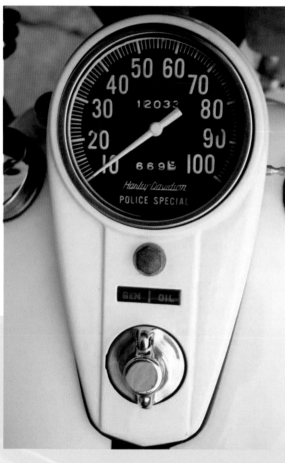

A clear and concise speedometer is essential for any speed cop. These were tested regularly.

There was some good news in 1953: Harley-Davidson celebrated its fiftieth birthday. A special logo was created to honour this achievement, which took the shape of a 'V,' paying tribute to the engine configuration that had served the company so well. Striking through the middle of the 'V' was a bar in which the company name was inscribed. Above and below the company name, '50 years' and 'American Made' was written. The 1954 models had one of these emblems placed on their front mudguard, although some badges varied slightly in their format.

The anniversary badge fitted to the front mudguard of this 1955 FLH, was in honor of the first V-Twin engine, which was still serving the company well.

The model K continued to be upgraded and became the KH in 1954, with a longer stroke, which pushed it from 45 cubic inches (750cc) to 54 cubic inches (883cc). A few more adjustments to increase the power output and the machine could finally reach 95mph (153kph), as yet unable to catch those Triumphs, but a little more patience and this too would happen. A factory-fitted Speed Kit and other goodies would be added the following year and the machine was redesignated KHK, now at last a much more competitive machine. There was little external difference between the KH and KHK, the lettering on the side of the oil tank identifying which model it was.

Uprated from the FL, the FLH (H standing for Hopped-up) was given more oomph! Power was now 60 hp and the bottom end of the engine was made stronger.

Speed King saddlebags were an optional extra and helped to set the bike off beautifully, especially in this colour.

One way of distinguishing the KH from the sportier KHK was by the lettering on the side of the oil tank.

The extra K on the designation, denoted the addition of a Speed kit, fitted at the factory and costing an extra US$68.

Yet another new design for the fuel tank paint work - this time a black slash of paint across it, which did attract attention.

The KHK was introduce in 1955 and was the hot rod machine to beat. It had good looks and plenty of go.

Top left: *The XLCH machine was inspired by the dealers, who wanted a light, agile machine to match the British twins.*

Bottom Left: *A basic instrument panel included a tachometer along with the speedometer.*

Centre: *Sportsters didn't come with electric starter, and so you had to be pretty careful when kicking one of these machines over!*

Model	1966 XLCH Sportster
Engine	Air Cooled, V-Twin, Four-Stroke
Ignition	Magneto
Power	40 hp
Bore x Stroke	3.00 x 3.81 in
Displacement	54cu.in /883cc
Fuel System	Single Tillotson diaphragm Carburettor
Transmission	Four-speed
Suspension	F: telescopic. R: twin shock
Brakes	Front/Rear: Drum
Weight	480 lbs
Top Speed	100 mph

1966 XLCH Sportster

Better still was to come and like many of its predecessors, the new machine improved as it aged. It has, and always did have, a niche of its very own. Taking its overall lines, and much of the technology found in the Model K, the new Sportster was presented in 1957. This was the machine that would match the British imports for top speed, and go on to beat them too with the XLH model. A new engine top-end was fitted, which included overhead-valves, a compression ratio of 7.1:5, allowing it to produce 40bhp at 5,500rpm. It was the following year that the machine was given a higher compression engine and designated XLH, giving it yet more power and a better top speed. A further XLCH model was also available, but this was classed as a scrambler and carried a small 2.2 gallon fuel tank, basically taken from the 125cc Hummer. How popular was the Sportster? Well the proof is in the pudding, as they say, and it is interesting to note that in 2007, fifty years of production is celebrated.

The year 1958 also saw another improvement with the introduction of the Duo Glide. The Hydra Glide, with just its front end being sprung, now had the addition of rear hydraulic suspension too, and became the Duo Glide. There were other improvements too, but fitting a rear swinging arm with shocks was significant. Ride comfort was greatly improved, although not all riders were convinced; this surely had to be better than just a sprung seat!

A fine example of a 1961 FL Duo Glide, with Panhead engine. It produced 60 hp from its 74 cubic inch engine.

Somewhat less attractive than the earlier instrumentation, although the large numbers were easy to read.

A well sprung rear end. The shocks now complemented the already well sprung seat.

As the 1950s turned into the 1960s, a new invader was quietly making itself known to the America motorcycle market – Japanese motorcycle companies. Japan was still reeling from the war but looking very seriously at easy-to-use commuter machines, that were reliable and comfortable. The American market was an obvious target to hit, as was the UK, with the possibilities of huge sales. As with the UK, the threat at this stage was barely noticed; the storm clouds were only just gathering.

In 1960, the Super 10 emerged, replacing both the Hummer and Model 165. It was equipped with a 165cc engine, which was the 'B' engine, that had previously been fitted to the 125cc Hummer. This was the nail in the coffin for the Model 165 'S' engine.

The engine of the Super 10, is a 6hp, single cylinder, air-cooled, 165cc, two stroke unit.

Looking more like a baked bean tin with air vents, this is the air filter for the 6 hp, Super 10s, single Tillotson carburettor.

The Super 10 engine was developed from the earlier Hummer 125cc engine, which had its roots back with the German DKW RT 125, acquired after the Second World War.

The Topper had some good qualities, such as large diameter wheels and automatic transmission. This machine is from 1962.

The Topper was introduced to compete in the fast growing scooter market of the period, but never really took off.

The little machine also had room for a passenger, foot pegs could be lowered to accommodate.

There was nothing too elegant or classy about the Topper, it was kept simple and easy, as shown with the instrumentation.

Model	1962 Topper
Engine	Air Cooled, Single-cylinder, Two-Stroke
Ignition	Magneto
Power	6 hp
Bore x Stroke	2 3/8 x 2 5/32 in
Displacement	10cu.in /64cc
Fuel System	Single Tillotson Carburettor
Transmission	'Scootaway' fully automatic
Suspension	Front: leading link fork
Brakes	Front/Rear: Drum
Weight	260 lbs
Top Speed	60 mph

Easily spotted here is the Aermacchi engine, although the Harley-Davidson name is stamped on the crankcase.

Built purely for the American market, this Sprint model was manufactured at the Aermacchi, Schiranna factory in Italy. There is little sign of Aermacchi on this machine, just the very distinctive engine. This is the slightly sportier H version, with a 246cc engine.

No such luxuries as electric starter for the little Sprint, although it was never the hardest machine to kick start.

The Harley-Davidson name is clearly stamped on the Aermacchi engine, which has a bore and stroke of 66 x 72mm, producing some 17hp.

Harley-Davidson in the meantime had decided to purchase half the stock of the Aermacchi motorcycle company, an Italian aeronautical concern which had also been making motorcycles since 1948. One of the first machines to be presented in 1960 was the Topper, a scooter-based machine that used a single-cylinder horizontal engine. Companies like Vespa and Lambretta were selling scooters by the dozens on the continent, where a real desire to own one of these machines had formed, and they were even having some success in the United States. Unfortunately the Topper would not take off in any way, shape or form, as the two other Italian scooters did. One machine that did take off though was the 250cc Sprint, launched in 1961. This particular model was also known as the Wisconsin, and although sold in Europe, it was in fact made for the American market. The Sprint went on to be developed in many different road-going versions, just as it did in

The telescopic front forks of the M50. Many new riders cut their teeth on machines like this one.

Built by Harley-Davidson's Italian subsidiary, Aermacchi, these machines were sold through Harley dealerships.

racing trim too. More Aermacchi-based models followed: a sportier Sprint H, the M50 – an attempt to cash in on the very small engine market that was being dominated by the Honda 50 – the M65 Leggero of 1968, the Rapido in the early 1970s, and of course the X-90 mini bike, often seen at race circuit pit areas. By the mid-1970s the Aermacchi concern was struggling financially and so the decision was made to dispose of it. It was finally returned to its mother country where a new motorcycle company, Cagiva, bought the concern out.

The X-90 was an uprated version of the 65cc model. It was a mini machine and ideal for younger riders to learn on.

The initial M50 was a 50cc machine, but was later enlarged to 65cc, producing 4.5hp with a top speed of 45 mph.

This is the little single-cylinder, air-cooled engine of the X-90. Note also the AMF addition to the fuel tank.

Only produced for one year in 1972, this is the Aermacchi Harley-Davidson model 350 TV/72.

The Aermacchi, 344cc, TV/72 engine, had a bore and stroke of 74 x 80 in., and produced 29hp at 7500 rpm.

A 1972 Aermacchi Harley-Davidson 'Aletta' 125. Clearly sitting higher than the standard machine, this is a motorcross bike.

The single-cylinder motor from the 'Aletta', was never quite good enough to compete with the Japanese and other European off-roaders.

Fitted between 1962 and 1967, this is the Tombstone speedometer used on the '66 Shovelhead.

No mistaking this model. This is the first of the Shovelhead machines for 1966.

Model	1966 FLH
Engine	Air Cooled, Four-stroke V-Twin
Ignition	Coil with points
Power	54 hp
Bore x Stroke	87 x 101 mm/3.44 x 3.97 in
Displacement	73.73cu.in /1208cc
Fuel System	Linkert Carburettor
Transmission	Four-speed
Suspension	Front: Telescopic fork
	Rear: Hydraulic shocks
Brakes	Front/Rear: Drum
Weight	783 lbs
Top Speed	100 mph/161kph

Shovelhead

By the mid-1960s, the sales of Harley machines were not as lively as they should have been, and it was decided that the time had come for a new model. The faithful Duo Glide, which had been introduced back in 1958, had given good service but was now to be replaced by the new Electra Glide model. With this, two very significant things took place. The Duo Glide was overhauled by the new Electra Glide, which would also become the last of the Panheads. This new machine became the first Big Twin to be equipped with an electric starter, which now allowed Harley owners to start their machines literally at the push of a button. Several changes were made to the frame to accommodate the large battery. The housing for this was positioned on the side of the machine, and could be easily identified by the large chrome cover. At the same time the oil tank was moved to the left-hand side. The toolbox was eliminated to make space for the battery, and the clutch and brake levers were made with ball-type ends for better grip. The following year also brought a further significant change with the introduction of the new Shovelhead engine.

1966 saw the Electra Glide fitted with a new set of aluminium heads, and rocker boxes that inspired the Shovelhead name.

The Electra Glide had grown in weight over the years, and the new modification to the engine helped to combat that.

An original 1965 Electra Glide, with electric start and the last of the Panhead engines, is now considered a rare machine. For 1966 the new Shovelhead engine was introduced to the Electra Glide, and so yet another Harley-Davidson legend was born. If there is a machine that people relate to Harley-Davidson, it surely has to be the Electra Glide. The new engine was not completely new; once again a top-end job had been done and there was a slight increase in power. This though also added to the ever-present vibration problem. Harley-Davidson riders are a hardy and faithful bunch though, and most accepted a bit of good news along with the bad.

This is a fine example of an original paint 1966 Shovelhead FLH model, with fibreglass saddlebags.

Instrumentation changed little, but the speedometer numbers were now being written in full.

This is a seat to be relied on. The Buddy seat is comfortable, and has an added handrail.

By the late 1960s it was obvious that things were not going well for Harley-Davidson, and although the Aermacchi connection had increased sales, there was no significant increase in profits. Financially, things were looking grim and although all measures were taken to stop a takeover of the company, this is exactly what happened. As ever with these situations, there were some courtroom histrionics, but at the end of the day, Harley-Davidson became a subsidiary of the American Machine and Foundry Company (AMF) in 1969.

Above: *Instrumentation on the 1969 Sportster, basic but functional. Just like the machine itself.*

Top Right: *The Sportster was introduced in 1957, and competed with the ever increasing numbers of British twins being imported.*

Bottom Right: *Four-stroke, air-cooled, V-Twin. 56 hp and a top speed of around 110 mph, this machine could move. Early models were kick-start, but this one has an electric starter.*

1977 FX Super Glide

Many will say that it was AMF who saw the company through bad times and actually saved it from the scrap heap. Others, on the other hand, just saw AMF as the bad guys and many still exclude that period as part of the Harley-Davidson history. Harsh, considering the amount of investment the AMF concern pumped into the company.

The Shovelhead engine is clearly seen here. The 74 cubic inch engine of the Super Glide, produced 65 hp and gave it a top speed of 105 mph (168 kph).

No mistaking the model, clearly marked on top of the headlamp. Instrumentation was fairly standard.

Whatever, the company did survive and in 1971 they introduced the FX Super Glide, an idea that came from Willie G., as he is known, the grandson of the original founder William Davidson. The Super Glide was a mix of Electra Glide engine and frame, fused to the Sportster front end. A Euro-style tail was probably the most unpopular part of the machine and was replaced the following year.

The FX Super Glide was introduced in 1971, and was a mix of rear FLH and front Sportster parts.

Designed by William G Davidson, the Super Glide was an attempt to produce a factory customised roadster.

This is the rather unfortunate rear tail and built-in light. It was unpopular with many riders and was soon discontinued.

The colours red, white and blue were very much identified with the AMF machines, but were in fact a patriotic gesture.

Just a beautiful looking machine, this is a 1971 FLH Special 1200cc model, with some style.

Some would call it overdone, but this special edition of the FLH was a classic of the early 1970s.

1971 FLH 1200 Special

Although faithful to the company for many years, the Shovelhead engine was seen by many faithful Harley riders as an AMF compromise.

This is a 1976, Limited production, Liberty edition of the FLH, with special metalflake paint to celebrate America's Centennial.

Instrumentation for the Limited edition machine changed little from the standard machine.

The large fairing of the FLH, an ideal place to put a patriotic gesture like the American eagle.

The top-box fits snugly behind the Buddy seat, which is equipped with single handrail.

Anybody who has seen that magical 1969 film 'Easy Rider', will recognise this machine right away. This is a 1999 adaptation of that bike, and what a beauty it is.

During this period, the American motorcycle rider had become very interested in customising his Harley-Davidson, influenced by films such as *Easy Rider*. Plenty of specialist outlets had also opened their doors to customers wanting to personalise their machines, with add-ons that the factory didn't supply. The Super Glide was aimed at the custom market, with many riders happy to have a factory-ready custom machine. Initially it was not a huge success, but as with so

The engine is an air-cooled, Harley-Davidson, Panhead V-Twin, with a capacity of 74 cubic inches, and producing 60 hp. It uses a four-speed transmission and can hit 90mph.

You would find it hard not to think this was one of the actual machines used in the film, it looks so authentic. Fonda, who rode the stars and stripes machine, which gained the nickname 'Captain America', was already a seasoned motorcyclist. He commented in an interview some time later, that it wasn't the easiest of machines to ride, and like all Harleys of the period, leaked oil from wherever it could!

many previous machines, the Super Glide went on to sell extremely well. Not long after AMF had taken over, a close review of the company and how it worked was instigated. This led to new systems being put in place and a planned strategy being organised for the future. Engines would be uprated for the present, but there would be a new range for the future – AMF were about to fund a product-led recovery of the now ailing company. Two more machines were to follow in 1977, both ideas from Willie G. First there was the XLCR Café Racer, a pretty mean-looking machine with its all-black paint job and Euro street-racer styling.

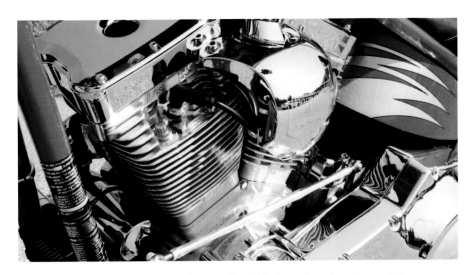

Big Dog Motorcycles have taken the standard V-Twin and produced something very special.

Big Dog Motorcycles of Wichita, Kansas, USA, started production in 1994, when this work of art was created.

If you want something different then this is the way to go. There is a vast selection of ways to be individual.

Model	1977 XLCR
Engine	Air Cooled, V-Twin, Four-Stroke
Ignition	Battery and coil
Power	68 hp
Bore x Stroke	81.4 x 96.8 mm
Displacement	61cu.in /1000cc
Fuel System	Single, 38mm, Keihin
Transmission	Four-speed
Suspension	Front telescopic forks. Rear twin shocks
Brakes	Front twin discs. Rear single disc
Weight	515 lbs
Top Speed	100 mph

The XLCR Café Racer styled Sportster was introduced in 1977, and was only available in one colour - black.

Today these machines are collectors' pieces, having only been made up to 1978. Finding one in good condition is difficult, as they were neglected and not well made.

1977 XLCR Café Racer

Unfortunately it was probably far too radical for the average Harley-Davidson rider, and sales never really took off. Today, many would also point out that the finish on the machine was also not up to the usual Harley-Davidson buyer expectation. Besides that, it was a good machine that was probably never properly appreciated by the American motorcyclist, and just two years after its debut, production came to an end. Today most of these machines are considered collectors' items and are often found in museums or private collections. As for the other 1977 model, this has become a real cult machine. The FXS Low Rider had a low seat height and featured drag bars, cast alloy wheels and a two-into-one exhaust system. It was exactly what its name depicted and fitted right into the style of the period, becoming an instant hit. The low, laid-back look is very much in evidence even today.

1977 FLH 1200 Electra Glide Classic

All glitz and glory. This is what people imagine when they think of a Harley-Davidson.
This is the FLH Electra Glide Classic of 1977.

Above: *Shiny pieces of metal hide the big 1200cc engine, used to pull the massive weight of the FLH.*

Top Right: *A riders-eye view of the instrument panel, which includes a built-in radio and cassette player.*

1978 was a year of celebration, not for sales but for the company, which had reached its seventy-fifth year in production. This was marked with the presentation of the 80 cubic inch (1340cc) Electra Glide, along with an anniversary edition of the FL1200, and an anniversary Sportster, painted black with gold pinstriping. The FLH Electra Glide was without doubt a good-looking machine and well equipped with saddlebags, luggage rack, running boards, fairing, and two extra side lights. Even though a heavyweight, and gaining no real power from the new engine, the added torque would make touring on this machine more comfortable and a lot more fun.

As the 1970s came to a close, a new machine was presented that was to be included within the cruiser/custom stable. The FXEF Fat Bob – 'Fat' because of the twin fuel tanks, 'Bob' because of the bobbed rear mudguard – came with a choice of 74 cubic inch (1200cc) or 80 cubic inch (1340cc) engine. Again this was a laid-back cruiser with high handlebars and stepped seat.

A beautiful looking 1981 FLH 80 HE. This was the first machine off the assembly line that was no longer under the AMF umbrella. The first one even had a gold oil dipstick.

Ten years had passed since AMF had taken control of the company and as yet the turnaround for profits was still not in view. There had been a steady line of machines produced which had sold reasonably well, but as yet the money that was needed to see the company through the future years was not forthcoming, at least not from profits. AMF had been funding quite a large chunk of the development work that was being carried out but with little return in the way of profits. They too were now getting impatient, and like all big businesses, they felt they had spent enough time and money on this project.

1980 was a year of vast activity with the introduction of the FLT Tour Glide, a machine that would incorporate a number of new and upgraded features. There was a newly designed frame, which incorporated a rubber-mounted, anti-vibration system, aimed at reducing any vibration from the engine. The engine now used electronic ignition, there were larger brakes, and a new Harley-Davidson five-speed gearbox. The front forks had had a considerable amount of work done on them, and there was now a five-gallon (twenty-two litre) fuel tank. There was no power increase but the bike was much more reliable, cleaner, and more comfortable, which now gave it a better chance to confront its main rival at the time, the Honda Goldwing.

Later in this same year the Sturgis model was introduced in honor of the motorcycle rally that takes place every year at Sturgis, South Dakota. The machine was the latest example of the Super Glide and given the designation FXB, the 'B' denoting the innovative new addition to the Harley-Davidson camp, a Kevlar belt, which would soon be used on all machines for primary and final drive purposes. The Sturgis was painted black, with chrome peripherals and a smattering of orange, as on the tank badge for example.

As mentioned earlier, 1980 was a busy year, and as if not enough new machinery and innovations had already been introduced, on came the FXWG Wide Glide, a Super Glide with Electra Glide front end. It also used the 80 cubic inch (1340cc) engine, which was now rapidly replacing the 74 cubic inch, in most Big Twin models – the 74 would be discontinued the following year.

Whilst all these events were being played out, back in the Harley-Davidson boardroom, unrest continued to smolder. AMF by now were losing interest in the company and wanted out. The matter was resolved in 1981, when a group of thirteen investors, led by Vaughn Beals and Willie G. Davidson, bought Harley-Davidson from AMF.

Model	1981 FLH 80 HE
Engine	Air Cooled, V-Twin, Four-Stroke
Ignition	Electronic
Power	60 hp
Bore x Stroke	89 x 108mm
Displacement	80cu.in /1340cc
Fuel System	Single 38mm Keihin Carburettor
Transmission	Four-speed
Suspension	F: telescopic. R: twin shock
Brakes	Front/Rear: Disc
Weight	752 lbs
Top Speed	95 mph

The new company officially started business on June 16, 1981, with a new slogan – The Eagle Flies Alone – to mark the occasion, and much celebrating was to follow. Once the jubilation was over, and reality set in, it was obvious that things had to change rapidly. Sadly, sales didn't suddenly take off, in fact they fell yet further, and by 1983 the company accounted for a mere 23 percent of the US large bike market. Not everything was doom and gloom though, as the new independent owners, themselves motorcyclists, were determined to turn the company fortunes around and make Harley-Davidson the force it once used to be. Led by Vaughn Beals, managers from Harley-Davidson were given an insight into the Japanese way of doing things when they visited the Honda factory in Ohio. Awe-struck by what they saw, they began to realise how far behind American industry, as a whole, was lagging. What they had seen needed to be instigated at Harley-Davidson, or the company surely would not survive.

One of the biggest problems was overstaffing, and this was part remedied right away with the reduction of two hundred clerical staff. With help from an outside consulting agency, who initiated pilot schemes such as 'just-in-time' statistical process control (better known at Harley-Davidson as 'Materials As Needed' – MAN), and other up-to-the-moment production controls, things started to change. Staff levels too, were further reduced from 3,800 to 2,200. The phrase 'lean and mean' comes to mind, and although a cliché, this is what needed to happen. Now the workers themselves took more responsibility for their work, and management took notice of what was happening on the shop floor. The quality issue, that was starting to tarnish the Harley-Davidson name, was being remedied, as was the reliability problem. But even with all this, there was no immediate payback –

These fringed leather saddlebags were part of the special equipment package, along with sprung seat and paint job, often referred to as 'peas and carrots'.

The official description of the colours was orange and olive drab. It didn't do the look of the machine any justice.

that would take time. In the meantime, Harley-Davidson made protests to the government regarding stockpiled, Japanese machines, that were being sold at cut-rate prices, and flooding an already declining motorcycle market. The complaints were finally upheld and the Reagan government imposed import taxes on incoming Japanese machines. Unfortunately this still left the Honda Goldwing untouched, as it was being produced in the home market. All the same Harley-Davidson decided to stick to what they were good at, the classic big American motorcycle. Make it clean and make it reliable, and surely those who had deserted the company would come back, and they did in even greater numbers!

One of the first machines to take Harley-Davidson into their new and unknown future was the FXR Super Glide II, which was presented in 1982 and came with a new frame, incorporating the rubber isolation system mounting the engine. The

'R' in the designation denoted this system, which also distinguished it from the standard FX.

This same year saw the twenty-fifth anniversary of the Sportster, and the company celebrated its birthday with a special edition, kitted out in black and silver paintwork. Although it still sold reasonably well, it was now facing, as were the other big machines, a new problem with emission laws, which were getting stricter each year. To come into line in 1982, the compression ratio was reduced, which in turn also reduced its power output and speed, which didn't help when it came to seeing off its rivals. Its main competitor at this time was the Honda CB900F, a machine that was considerably faster and cheaper to buy.

It was 1983 when the Harley Owners Group (HOG) was formed, an organisation set up and sponsored by Harley-Davidson, to make owners around the world more aware of what the company could offer them, and to allow their dealerships

to be in better contact with the company itself. Today it is probably the biggest brand-related club in the world, with some half a million members, and chapters all over the globe. Besides promoting the name of Harley-Davidson and all its various products, it also organises events such as ride-outs. It was also during this period that the company started scrutinising more closely the use of its trademark and copyrighted material. Today it vigorously polices all its logos, names, and other Harley-Davidson related material, to the point that they even attempted to secure a trademark protection against their exhaust note, in 1994. After six years of legal to-ing and fro-ing, with no real result, Harley-Davidson withdrew the request but claimed it had won in the court of public opinion.

Only produced in limited numbers, the XR1000 is regarded by many as one of Harley-Davidson's best motorcycles ever.

The bike was aggressively fast, but manufacturing was discontinued after only two years of limited production. Today it is a highly desirable rare machine.

1983 XR1000

The VR1000 has, as its title denotes, a 60.84 cubic inch (1000 cc), V-Twin engine, that can produce 71hp, and a top speed of 125mph (201kph).

Based on the standard Sportster, the engine is highly modified. It was fitted with the cylinder heads and twin Dell'Orto carburettors from the XR750 race bike.

Evolution

The year 1984 was one to remember: it was the year that the new Evolution engine was presented. This was a make-or-break time for Harley-Davidson and it would be the Evolution engine that would play the biggest part in the survival of the company. Although not a completely new unit, it had evolved over a number of years, using the enormous experience acquired by members of the company. Still based on the trusty V-twin configuration, this new engine was to be lighter, tighter, stronger, and more flexible, whilst at the same time carrying on the traditions and expectations of the company.

In 1983 the XR-1000 was introduced, a much requested street version of the XR-750 race machine, and although not a great success as a street machine, the engine became the basis of the infamous 'Lucifer's Hammer' race bike. Dick O'Brien took the same engine and fitted it to a road racing chassis and added special suspension, special brakes, and a fairing, along with a few other trick

Model	1988 FLHTC Electra Glide Classic
Engine	Air Cooled, V-Twin, Four-Stroke
Ignition	Electronic
Power	65Hhp
Bore x Stroke	88.8 x 108.0 mm (3.5 x 4.3 inches)
Displacement	80cu.in /1340cc
Fuel System	Single 38mm Keihin Carburettor
Transmission	Five-speed
Brakes	Front: Duel disc. Rear: Single disc.
Weight	771.6 lbs
Top Speed	93.2 mph (150.0 kph)

parts. Jay Springsteen and Gene Church would place the machine squarely in the history books after wins at Daytona and the BOTT (Battle of The Twins) series. To many riders the XR-1000, at some $7,000, was just too expensive. Right now Harley-Davidson needed to recapture its grassroots riders, those that were looking for a classic Harley at the right price. This came in the form of the XLX 61, a cut-price Sportster that would help to bring riders back to the showrooms and revitalise the Harley-Davidson name. By 1984 the new Evo engine was starting to take its place in the Harley-Davidson history books and one of the first machines to proudly bear the new engine was the FXST Softail. Although at a glance you would also assume that this machine had a rigid-rear, a closer look would disclose shock absorbers tucked neatly under the transmission; now the machine had suspension! So many good things were happening – fitted to the limited edition FLHX Electra Glide of 1984 was the last of the solid mounted Shovelhead engines, whilst the FXEF Fat Bob of the same year bore the last of the Shovelhead engines in the Super Glide series, and by 1985 all Big Twin machines were fitted with the new Evolution engine. A radical change had taken place, and even though it had been gradual, it had sharply improved the quality and reliability of the machines, as well as improving sales. By the end of the 1980s, the company was once again making generous profits, had regained a large chunk of the market share it had previously lost, and even the supply of machines to the police departments of America had picked up – a lucrative market that had been lost to the incoming Japanese machines such as Kawasaki.

Made in a limited edition, this is machine number 703 of 850. It is an 85th anniversary model for 1988.

This is the 80 cubic inch engine of this beautiful Softail Classic, as verified on the air filter cover.

Classed as a Custom cruiser, this FLSTC has had a special carburettor intake cover fitted. It not only looks good but also helps the engine to breathe better. The instrumentation (left) is standard for the model and period.

By 1988 the Sportster had gone through some changes too; its 883cc model had been joined by an 1100cc version and by 1988 that too had been increased to a whopping 1200cc. This same year yet another bit of Harley-Davidson heritage was reintroduced. The FXSTS Softail Springer was presented with Springer-style forks. Although these forks dated back forty years, the company had spent time on the computer reconfiguring them for a modern age, and then when they were happy that they would work, they fitted them to the FXSTS.

The company had gone through such a bad time that many had never imagined it would still be trading in 1988. In fact the corner had been turned and it could now boast a modern, reliable, and comprehensive line-up of machines. Those who doubted the company during the bad days now had to eat their words, and 1988 saw Harley-Davidson celebrate their eighty-fifth anniversary, introducing a new badge for the celebrations.

Ending the 1980s was the FLHTC, a Classic Electra Glide kitted out for comfort and long rides. As if the rider's seat wasn't padded enough, the passenger seat now also had built-in arm rests. There was more than enough space for luggage in the panniers and top-box, and it now came with self-cancelling direction indicators. As if this wasn't enough, 1990 saw the introduction of the FLTC Ultra Classic Tour Glide, a sophisticated machine with built-in CB radio, intercom, stereo, and even cruise control. The addition of three disc brakes was much appreciated by riders – this was a big machine to stop in a hurry. In the meantime Willie G., had been busy organising more machines, and who would have imagined one named Fat Boy! This FLSTF had a top speed of 114 mph (183kph), the front and rear wheels were of the dish type and used the now regular belt drive. It was distinguishable by its silver paintwork, wide mudguards, and fat tires.

The early nineties saw the return of a limited-run Sturgis. The FXDB Dyna Glide Sturgis now used the Evo engine, and had a new chassis, which had the advantage of being designed on a computer. From one limited edition machine to another. The 1992 FXDB Daytona was a celebration of the Daytona 200, which by 1991 had been running for fifty years.

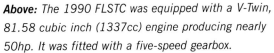

Above: *The 1990 FLSTC was equipped with a V-Twin, 81.58 cubic inch (1337cc) engine producing nearly 50hp. It was fitted with a five-speed gearbox.*

Top Right: *Seen through the wire wheel is the single front brake disc, and on the mudguard is confirmation of the machines' heritage.*

Right: *Almost as it came out of the factory. The proud owner has removed the engine on more than one occasion to keep it running at peak performance.*

The Daytona was seen as the first Harley-Davidson with real pearl paintwork – gold pearl-glo and indigo blue metallic – and the fuel tank wore a fiftieth-year anniversary badge. The following was yet another anniversary, the ninetieth year of Harley-Davidson, and all machines carried a special ninetieth-year badge to celebrate. There were celebrations not only in Milwaukee, but around the world. Special bike outings turned up in Milwaukee, parties were thrown, and all kinds of motorcycling events took place to celebrate this great achievement. At the same time six Anniversary Edition machines were presented, customised with silver and charcoal paintwork, and with serialised license plates and cloisonné emblems on the tank. The year 1993 saw another US company in some difficulty. Eric Buell, ex-racer and already well known to Harley-Davidson, having bought many of their engines, had struck up business on his own. He had also worked for the company on their rubber-mounted frame, but then left in 1985, to build racing machines. One of the machines he built, made a name for itself in the BOTT (Battle of The Twins) race series, and in fact was given the designation RR1000 Battle Twin. Once fitted with the new Evolution engine it became the RR1200, and a stripped down version was designated RS. The bike carried a lot of new ideas, which Buell himself had been instrumental in designing. A birdcage-type frame, with rubber mounts at the top, was designed to carry the V-twin engine. A Works Performance shock absorber was positioned under the engine, acting as the damper for the rear wheel, and the exhaust silencer was also placed under the engine. Buell, though, lacked the financial backing to go ahead with new projects, and so in 1993

The front wheel of the Buell RR1000 Battletwin, mostly enclosed in bodywork to help with aerodynamics.

Simple but effective instrumentation, makes for easy reading at speed.

Harley-Davidson acquired 49 percent of the Buell Motorcycle Company Inc. In 1995 the first result of the partnership was presented in the shape of the Buell S2 Thunderbolt, a sports machine that could be used for touring, with the addition of saddle boxes. Again the distinctive under-slung shock absorber and exhaust silencer were also evident.

The Harley-Davidson FLHR Road King was also introduced in 1995, and bore a new five-gallon tank with speedometer and digital odometer fitted on the top. Modern technology was mixed with some very good-looking 1960s retro, for example the white-wall tires, fly screen, low-drawn mudguards, and detachable passenger seat. Fuel injection and electronic engine management also appeared at this time, all helping to comply with the tight emission control laws that were now creeping into California and Europe.

Fully enclosed bodywork hides the powerful 998cc Harley-Davidson engine. The name Battletwin, is derived from the Battle of the Twins race series, for which it was entered.

Buell too were ready to present their latest machine for 1996, the model S1 Lightning, a pure sports machine that shared the frame form of the S2 but otherwise was a new machine. The bike was fitted with an all-new small screen, four-gallon fuel tank, and short and stubby rear mudguard. There was a rather large airbox on the side, which some long-legged riders couldn't get on with. Just a year later, along came the M2 Cyclone, a more usable machine with a better price tag. A decent size seat, and for those who had problems with the S1 airbox, this one was shaped to give taller riders more legroom. There was also an X1

The RR1100 became the RR1200, when fitted with the Evolution engine.
It later lost a considerable section of its bodywork after becoming the RSS1200.

The radical but typical Buell suspension, can be spotted clearly under the engine of the S1.

The Buell S1 White Lightning was one of the most exciting sports machines on the market when it was announced in the mid 1990s.

Instrumentation for the S1 is extremely user-friendly, clear, clean and comprehensive.

The S1 uses a Harley 1203cc, air-cooled, OHV, pushrod V-Twin engine that is much modified. The air intake box can often be a nuisance to riders with long legs.

With the 1998 FLSTS Heritage Springer, Harley-Davidson have resurrected the dead.
The machine takes so many features that were seen back in the 1948 period.

Lightning added to the pack, which received rave reviews. It was without doubt very fast and exciting, but came with a pretty steep price tag. For 1998 the new Thunderstorm engine was introduced by Buell, initially in S1W White Lightning machines. Similar in design to the original S1, it also featured a carbon fiber rear mudguard, stronger colours, and of course the new engine. It wasn't long before the Thunderbolt models were also fitted with the new engine too. A new Research and Development Centre was opened in 1999, located just adjacent to the East Troy factory in Wisconsin.

Having bought nearly half the Buell Company back in 1993, Harley-Davidson decided to claim another 49 percent of the company in 1998, leaving just 2 percent, which they would also purchase in 2003.

Springer front forks have been around since 1988 but much work had to be done to bring them up to the present day standards.

The 1997 Heritage Springer is an impressive looking machine, with some good detail work. A tombstone style taillight and front running light have been added to rear and front mudguards.

Like many parts of the machine, the instrumentation is now fully chromed, complimenting the handlebars and front suspension beautifully.

1999 Sportster 1200

Sitting pert and pretty is the 1999 Sportster. It uses the standard belt final drive,
and has front and rear disc brakes.

The machine is based around the 73.20 cubic inch (1200cc), V-twin engine, and has a top speed of 110mph (176kph).

At the top on the air cleaner cover is the engine size, and below on the gearbox cover is a distinctive number 5, denoting the gears that are available.

The rear end of the 1200cc Sportster, showing the single brake disc and caliper.

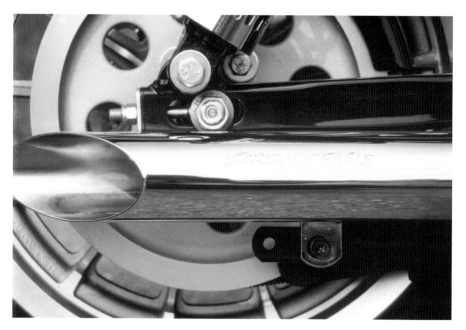

Behind the well sliced silencer is the belt final-drive wheel. The power transmitted through this via the drive-belt must be phenomenal.

Twin Cam 88

There were more important things happening in 1999 though, and the introduction of the new Twin Cam 88 (88 cubic inch, 1450cc) engine was at the top of the list. The Evo engine had finally run its race and had by now been overtaken by its rivals.

The Twin Cam 88 was a 45-degree, V-twin, with twin cams incorporated, which were chain-driven. Many asked why, being so close to the crank, they weren't cog-driven. The reason seems to be the noise factor – making sure that the unit sounded like an authentic Harley-Davidson, and cog-driven cams create a noise that is not compliant to the Harley-Davidson motorcycle. Whatever, the new engine became known as the Fathead, and although it had increased power output by 10–25 percent, the main focus had been on reliability and serviceability.

Introduced in 1999 for the year 2000, the FXSTD Softail Deuce was fitted with the new Twin Cam 88B engine. This was the next stage of the 88 engine, introduced in 1999. The 'B' featured two counter-rotating balancers to help cancel out primary engine vibration, therefore enhancing the reliability of the rigid mounted engine. The advertising explained that it was kitted out with a host of stylish details designed to set it apart from the crowd. Indeed it had chrome forks, a first for the company, and also had a stretched fuel tank, another first for the company. The rear mudguard housed an inlaid rear light, and there was an extra-wide rear tire.

This is the 2004 FXSTI softail standard. A basic machine that can be tailored to either his or her specification. Choose from the many accessories available.

The new Twin Cam 88B engine, used in the FXSTI of 2004. This is an air-cooled, two valves per cylinder, 1449cc unit.

The V-Twin engine uses a five-speed transmission unit, with belt final drive, controlled by a nine-plate, wet clutch.

July of 2003 saw Buell announce the arrival of the new XB12R Firebolt, a bigger brother to the XB9R, with more oomph and better handling characteristics. This was not a machine for the faint at heart!

To pander to the younger generation, who craved something different and perhaps something more exciting, Buell introduced the Blast in 2000. This was an easy to use, easy to maintain bike that housed a single-cylinder, air-cooled, 492cc engine. At the top end of the range for 2002, was the introduction of the Buell Firebolt XB9R. Fitting right into the Street Fighter category, Buell introduced this as a Sport Fighter. It was fitted with a new 45-degree, V-twin engine, equipped with DDFI fuel injection, and produced some 95hp. The new frame doubled up as the fuel tank also, and with the fuel sitting very low in the frame, it was designed to enhance the overall handling. The swing-arm also had a secondary function, as the oil reservoir.

Model	2004 XB12R FIREBOLT
Engine	Air Cooled, V-Twin, Four-Stroke
Ignition	Electronic
Power	100hhp
Bore x Stroke	88.9 x 96.82 mm (3.5 x 3.8 inches)
Displacement	73.70cu.in /1203cc
Valves	OHV, 2vpc
Fuel System	49mm Downdraft DDFI fuel injection
Transmission	Five-speed
Brakes	Front/Rear: Single disc
Weight	850 lbs

Buell XB12R

Long smooth looks, with plenty of chrome; the 2001 V-Rod was a completely different machine than had ever been seen before from the Harley-Davidson stable.

Revolution

The next machine to come out of the Harley-Davidson stable took most people by surprise. It was radically different to anything that had been produced before, and would introduce a whole new line of machines for the future. The year 2001 saw the presentation of the brand-new V-Rod, the first member of a performance cruiser family. The machine, initially presented in silver with lashings of chrome, was fitted with the new Revolution engine, which too was something different. This is a water-cooled, 60-degree, V-twin, with dual overhead camshafts and four-valve heads. The Revolution engine is a result of the VR-1000 Superbike race program and was developed by Harley-Davidson's Powertrain Engineering team, in conjunction with Porsche engineering in Stuttgart, Germany.

A revolution had truly begun with the introduction of the all-new V-Rod model, and its Revolution engine, anodised aluminium body panels, and polished aluminium solid-disc wheels.

The machine itself was low, sleek, and beautifully finished off. The combination of rubber isolation connections and balance shafts made the ride silky smooth, and the dished wheels set the bike off beautifully. Further versions would follow, with more advanced features catering to specific requirements.

2003 was a momentous year for Harley-Davidson in which it celebrated one hundred years of manufacturing. In Milwaukee, Labor Day weekend was turned into a four-day Harley-Davidson event, as thousands of people came to watch and participate in a 10,000-motorcycle parade through the city. A party was held on the shores of Lake Michigan, with artists performing in front of 150,000 spectators, who had been given free tickets, and even President Bush sent a congratulatory message. Milwaukee wasn't the only place to be taken over by the celebrations, in fact there were parties all over the world to celebrate one hundred years of this American icon. As in previous celebratory years, 2003 models were kitted out with distinctive badges, trim, and special paint.

2003 was a momentous year for Harley-Davidson. The company had seen depression, ownership change and general despair. It had overcome all that, and more, and was now ready to celebrate 100 years of production.

This anniversary Electra Classic tells the story on its air cleaner cover: Harley-Davidson 100 years of great motorcycles. Street parties happened all over the world to celebrate this incredible achievement.

2003 Anniversary Road King

Fully equipped anniversary Road King. Even the rider has a backrest, let alone the passenger!

No explanation needed here. Some would never have believed, just a few years ago, that Harley-Davidson would still be around in the new millennium.

The 2003 FLHR Road King was a pretty machine. It weighed 760.6 lbs, was 96.1 inches long and had a seat height of 29.1 inches.

The Road King used a 88.42 cubic inch (1449 cc) engine and came in Vivid black, gunmetal pearl, luxury rich red pearl, white pearl (as seen here) and luxury blue pearl.

2005 VRSC V-Rod

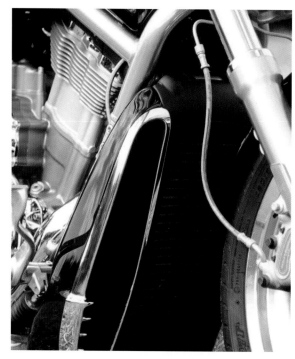

As the next few years came and went, models were improved and added to, so that by 2007 the V-Rod range was just one range that was by now outstanding. The original is still there but is now joined by the VRSCD Night Rod, which has slotted disc wheels and shiny chrome engine covers. The VRSCDX Night Rod Special, is literally that, special! The 120hp that it churns out gives the fat rear tire plenty to think about, and the black paintwork and silver silencers make it stand out from the others in the range. These are just two of the new V-Rod range to be seen alongside a mouthwatering selection of other machines in the Harley-Davidson stable.

The V-Rod is the most awarded Harley-Davidson ever. Its silver leaf aluminium frame and chrome engine trim can be easily spotted here. The Revolution engine is water-cooled and has a radiator with twin vortex air scoops, surrounded by chrome.

A chrome, clamshell instrument housing is neatly fitted between the drag-style handlebars. The dials may look clumsy, but are in fact very clear and easy to read.

The 1130cc Revolution engine fits neatly into the silver leaf frame, with the large bore exhausts feeding neatly away from the two barrels.

Possibly the best looking Harley-Davidson to date. The 2005 VRSCA uses an eighteen inch, dished rear wheel, and nineteen inch, dished front wheel.

Part of the Dyna series, this is the 2005 FXDLI Low Rider, and low it is! The forks are raked at a 32 degree angle and the seat is set at a height of 640mm. With the pulled-back bars and mid-mounted foot controls, this is not a difficult machine to ride.

The tank-mounted speedometer and tachometer, keep you informed of how the Twin Cam 88 engine is performing.

Sportsters now range from the 883 custom, to a fiftieth anniversary model, which is only made in limited numbers. The Dyna range now spans from the Super Glide, through the Super Glide Custom, Street Bob, Low Rider, and at nearly US$17,000, the beautiful-looking Wide Glide. There is a choice of eight Softails, ranging from the Standard to the Heritage Softail Classic. Then the tourers, just a glut to choose from – Road King, Street Glide, Road Glide, and Electra Glide – they are all there in various guises and make-up. The Buell operation too is increasing its selection of machines with both the Lightning and Firebolt series. There is now a new machine that seems as happy on the fast straight roads as it is on rough back-roads. The Ulysses has increased suspension travel and higher and more upright handlebars. The single-cylinder Blast is still there too, now even more refined than before.

The 2006 FLSTFSE, Screamin Eagle, 'Fat Boy', has heaps of power in the Twin Cam 103B engine. There is plenty of chrome and a custom paint job with Road Winder wheels to give it all-round good looks.

A true touring motorcycle, the 2006 Harley-Davidson FLHTCI Electra Glide Classic features the King Tour-Pak rear luggage box and passenger backrest.

Like so many of the other motorcycle companies, clothing too is now also a big part of the two operations. Entering any Buell/Harley-Davidson dealership, you will find a huge selection of traditional and modern clothing, helmets, sunglasses, boots, calendars, and any manner of goods.

The future of Harley-Davidson looks bright and the thought of another one hundred years is easily imagined. It's unlikely that the faithful V-twin will be around then, and one can only wonder what motorcycle engines will look like in another one hundred years – if motorcycles still exist then!

Comprehensive engine instrumentation, mudguard and saddlebag trim, and chrome engine covers. The 2006 Electra Glide Classic also has a 40-watt Advanced Audio System by Harman/Kardon.

The FLHTCUI Ultra Classic Electra Glide, is regarded as the ultimate touring motorcycle in the Harley-Davidson range. Electronic Sequential Port Fuel Injection, passenger sound system, CB radio and intercom system, cruise control and full instrumentation are all standard for this classic 2006 machine.

Yes, the new FLHXI Street Glide also has Sequential Port Injection for its power plant.

The 2006 Street Glide is fitted with the familiar 1450cc V-Twin engine, which gets a black and chrome finish treatment. Fairing-mount mirrors are also a great improvement.

This is the 2006, new touring family member, the FLHXI Street Glide. Not only are the luggage bags colour matched, their closing/locking systems are too.

For 2007, Harley-Davidson launched the Twin Cam 96/96B engine. This was an all-new, larger displacement, 1584cc Big Twin engine

First seen at Intermot in Cologne earlier in 2006, the UK Motorcycle show viewing of the new Harley-Davidson XR1200, was to gauge media and public reaction to the new style machine.

The VRSC family of liquid-cooled Powercruiser and Roadster motorcycles, had two new models joining them in 2007. This is the menacing VRSCDX Night Rod Special.

Daytona

The traditional Daytona Bike Week, held in Florida, USA, saw its 65th anniversary in March of 2006. Even though some 500,000 bikers turn up every year, many of them don't realise that this is not just a 'show your machine off' event. There is much more going on: drag racing, flat track racing, supercross, and 750 SuperSport races, to name a few. In the early days, Daytona racing was carried out mainly on the sand, Harley-Davidson ruled, and their machines won all the prizes. Today Harley-Davidson don't race that much, but there is still plenty to do at Daytona. You can ride the Loop, check out the vendors, and even get your bike blessed at the 'Blessing of the Bikes' ceremony. Then of course there is the annual Harley-Davidson Parade, where owners take the greatest pride in showing off their fabulous, glittering machines.

Daytona is a meeting where you will encounter all kinds of bikes. Some will have been professionally customised, others just modified by their owners.

OK so it's leather, but probably not enough of it! Then again, if you've got it, flaunt it, as they say!

What was the attraction back in 1937 that enticed people to Daytona Beach. The hard sand, the warm winter days or just the excitement of that first motorcycle race on the beach. Whatever it was, it still attracts thousands today.

Sturgis

Each year, literally hundreds of thousands of motorcyclists head for Sturgis, in South Dakota, USA. This again is an annual event which has been going since 1938, and which keeps growing in popularity. Many consider this as the Mecca of the motorcycling world, and attend without fail every year. It started with a small group of Jackpine Gypsies Motorcycle Club members, who were keen to attract tourists to their town. Today it is one of the biggest motorcycle meets in the world, and unless you book your accommodation a year ahead, you may well be sleeping rough! The name was changed to Sturgis Rally and Races in 1992, although most people still just call it Sturgis.

Sturgis is a special place for motorcyclists. Steeped in history and situated in the scenic Black Hills, it is a place where motorcyclists can enjoy camaraderie with their friends and freedom on the open road.

A visit to Sturgis would not be complete without a trip down the historic Main Street. Five blocks are open to motorcycle traffic only, creating a sea of bikes and people.

People ride their machines up and down the street, seeing the sights and being seen. There aren't just colourful bikes, the people can be too.

Along with the riders of the period, it was machines like these that gave the Harley-Davidson racing team, the superiority that is so rightly deserved. The Wrecking Crew were a formidable force, and one that was never matched.

The Wrecking Crew

Initially, Harley-Davidson were reluctant to join the world of racing. The founders considered it an unnecessary extravagance and thought it better to concentrate on the job in hand – producing good machinery for their faithful clients. As time went on though, and seeing their main rivals Indian getting more than ample publicity through racing, they reluctantly joined in. Although success would not come right away, when it did come, it was an adventure that nobody could ever have dreamed about. Since then the company has contributed to all forms of racing, initially with the main emphasis on board track racing, then dirt track events, which were favoured in the United States, compared to tarmac road racing European-style.

Early on, Walter Davidson had dabbled in racing, but mainly with endurance events, which generally gave account of the machine that was being ridden. The thinking behind this was that if the motorcycle could go the distance, then people would see that it was a reliable and well built machine, and would therefore be more likely to buy it. It became more and more evident though, that winning prestigious races could enhance the profile of a company even further, and Harley-Davidson realised they could no longer ignore the extra publicity that could be gained by competing in these races. Therefore in 1913 the company set up a racing department, after hiring William Ottaway, the man who had been at the heart of the Thor Company racing success. Although Thor was not a major player on the racing scene, Ottaway influence and expertise had gained them some good wins both with endurance and dirt track racing. He was employed to work alongside William Harley, in setting up the new racing department, and soon the two men set about refining the Harley V-twin engine for racing.

The first racer to be pitched against the likes of Indian and Henderson was a machine derived from the Model 10E, using the 61 cubic inch, 1000cc V-twin engine. A handful of machines were built for 1914, but the following year, with the influence of Ottaway and his pit crew management organisation, the team

Typical posters of the period, show the events that Harley-Davidson dominated, and the spectators just loved to attend in their thousands. It made for a great day out and some very exciting racing.

The drop handlebars allowed the rider to tuck down behind them - no fairing here to keep the wind off. There were no front or rear brakes either.

1914 marked the first year that the Harley-Davidson Motor Company entered the 'racing game'. This is a factory special A Motor racer. Note the 'non skid' tyres.

Ottaway developed and improved valve timing, incorporated larger intake ports and carburettor. His engine technology was the foundation for a reliable F-head configuration.

began to be more prominent. In the April, Otto Walker won the Venice, California, three hundred mile road race, followed in by another Harley-Davidson rider, Leslie Parkhurst. All the major manufacturers were there and the race was given good coverage by the media. Another prestigious race held not long after was the Dodge City three hundred mile race, and here Harley-Davidson took six of the seven top positions. In just a couple of years, Harley-Davidson's racing team had come a very long way, and by the end of 1915, the team were a force to be reckoned with, and the competition found themselves with a new and very strong opposition.

Limited quantities of racing machines were developed by William Ottaway, who challenged the competition with fast machines and team organisation. Venice, California hosted the test bed for his effort and by mid 1915 the media expounded on the performance of the 'Wrecking Crew.'

This factory special A Motor racer, featured magneto ignition, pedal crash for starting, a rear wheel clutch and rivetted long distance fuel tank. The production numbers of this model are unknown; however, to date only three exist.

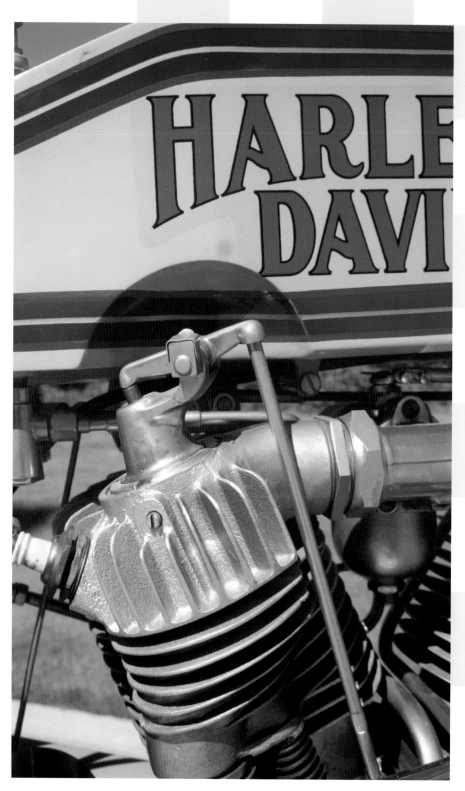

The Speed Roadster was in fact a competition machine with street equipment - similar to what we might call a production racer today.

It used a V-Twin, four-stroke, air-cooled, 60.33 cubic inch (997cc) engine. It produced 16hp and used a single Schebler carburettor.

Above: Harley-Davidson advertising at the time, said that you could ride this machine to a speed event, compete, and then ride it home again. These machines are very rare to find now, and this particular example could be the only one in existence.

Left: The engine had bore and stroke measurements of 84 x 90mm, with the classic 'F' head layout of overhead inlet and side exhaust valves.

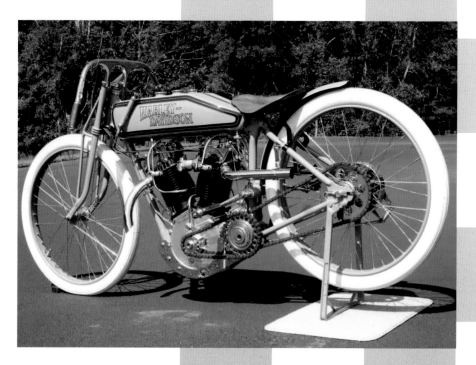

It would be difficult to find a machine in better condition than this one. This is a beautiful example of a 1916, 8-valve racer. The motor is a 61 cubic inch, four valves per cylinder, V-Twin. Only six of these machines were made in this year.

1916 8-valve Board Track racer

The handlebars and seat on these racing machines were fixed at their lowest settings, so that the rider could crouch down as far as he could, and slipstream through the air. This machine has a top speed of 120 mph - pretty frightening to think of that alone - then take into consideration that it has no brakes! Note the racing carburettor protruding from the side.

This 1920, 8-valve, board track race machine, is an incredible example, of what many would say, was the most sophisticated experimental twin, ever produced by Harley-Davidson.

Single speed transmission, with no clutch. These machines had to be pulled to start them, and when they got going you knew all about it!

This is the powerplant used in the 8-valve racer. An air-cooled, V-Twin, overhead valve, four stroke unit. It was machines like this that gave the company race team the nickname 'Wrecking Crew'.

The rear of the machine had rigid suspension, in other words nothing! The front though had sprung forks and Hartford damper. You can't even begin to imagine how uncomfortable the riders must have felt, lap after grueling lap.

The start of 1916 saw the emergence of the Wrecking Crew, a name given to the Harley-Davidson racing team by journalists of the period, to describe how Ottaway team would always wreck any other team's chances of winning - they were formidable and dominated racing during this period. The Crew went through changes but there were some who became legends, such as Jim Davis, Ralph Hepburn, Fred Ludlow, Otto Walker, Maldwyn Jones, and Ray Weishaar. This year the Crew wrapped up fifteen national championships, and there seemed no end to the victorious run. The machine that was now being used was the celebrated eight-valve racer, an engine that had been designed using all the experience Ottaway had, with some help from Englishman Harry Ricardo. Like all new engines it took time to sort out, but when it finally got into its stride, it helped the riders to dominate the racing scene like never before.

Unfortunately, the run had to come to an end as the First World War intervened and all racing was stopped, and would not commence for another three years. Once life got back to normality, the record breaking and victories started again.

This machine is believed to be one of only eight built, and the asking price at the time was an astronomical US$1500. This helped Harley-Davidson to keep control over these machines, and campaign them purely for the factory team riders.

1920 8-valve Board Track racer

The 8-valve machine used a single Schebler carburettor for delivery of fuel to the V-Twin, 999cc engine.

Shown here are two of the eight valves, from the V-Twin engine. These were pushrod activated, and there were four valves per cylinder.

The 8-valve racer on home ground. A display at the Barber Vintage Motorsports Museum, houses this wonderful and rare machine for all to see and enjoy.

Right: The transmission on the Peashooter was single speed countershaft direct drive, with no clutch. Stopping was often a problem as there were no brakes!

Below: These little 350cc machines, were very popular in speedway events in Europe and Australia. They were given their nickname 'peashooter' due to the staccato bark of the exhaust note.

Red Parkhurst scored at Daytona in 1919, Ray Weishaar won the race at Marion, Indiana, and endurance race records were broken too by Harley-Davidson dealer Hap Scherer, who took the new Sport Twin on the long-distance races, such as the New York to Chicago run and the Canada to Mexico, 'three flags' run.

The team entered the 1921 racing season but this was to be the last for some time. Neither riders nor Ottaway were told until the last race of the year, which left some pretty unhappy riders and some bad feeling towards the company. Following this, a few of the riders managed to take part as private entrants or with other teams. Victories were being taken abroad too; for example in England, Freddie Dixon wrapped up the 1000cc world championship at Brooklands, riding a Harley-Davidson. This was a circuit that had seen a Harley-Davidson as the first motorcycle to run at 100mph just two years earlier.

1929 Peashooter

The engine was an air-cooled, single-cylinder, four-stroke unit, with overhead valves operated via pushrods. The 350cc class was introduced to racing in 1926, to help make dirt track racing safer. It wasn't long though before the 350s were going as fast as the 500s.

Suspension consisted of none at the rear, or rigid as it was known. The front was telescopic fork. The whole machine weighed 185lbs.

As the glory days of track racing faded, American motorcycle companies looked towards hill-climb events. This is a beautifully restored 1920 DAH 750, of which less than twenty were made.

The heart of the DAH machine was an entirely new 45 cubic inch (750cc) overhead valve engine, with a single exhaust valve feeding two exhaust ports.

Can you even begin to wonder what it was like to do 95 mph on a machine like this, with no brakes, no clutch and no transmission! The Peashooter was instrumental in giving Harley-Davidson the reputation it gained in motorcycle racing.

This 1930 peashooter is a one-off machine, and unlike the other Peashooter racers, it has a larger 500cc, OHV engine fitted.

This particular WR racer has some history to it. The bike is in fact one of a kind, as it was raced by Daytona legend Babe Tancrede, winner of the Daytona 200 in 1940.

The 1946 WR 750cc racing machine. It was powered by a 38hp, V-Twin, side valve engine with MR4 racing carburettor, and had a three-speed transmission unit.

Sitting quite low to the ground, the little WR certainly has plenty of grunt, and could reach a frightening 105 mph.

With the advent of the AMA (American Motorcycle Association) in 1924, and their attempts to slow race machines down following a spate of dreadful accidents, Harley-Davidson produced two new single-cylinder machines, initially for the export market in England and Australia. The introduction of these two models led to the development and introduction of the celebrated Peashooter race machine, used extensively during the 1920s.

Probably the best known racer at the time was Joe Petrali, who became yet another legend in the Harley-Davidson story. One of the last great Class A racing stars, Petrali competed in board track, dirt track, speed records, and hill climbs, and won forty-nine AMA national championship races.

1949 WR

The WR was a special build competition machine, base on the WL street model. There were two versions, a dirt track racer and a TT model for scrambles, although the machine was also used for other types of racing too. Features included a chrome-moly frame and aluminium cylinder heads. Power rating was 38hp and it was capable of a 100mph top speed.

According to the Harley-Davidson data book, the KHRM was suitable for off-road scrambles or trials competitions. They were also used in enduro racing, such as the Jack Pine endurance race in Michigan, USA. The 54 cubic inch (883cc), air-cooled, V-Twin, engine produced some 55 hp. it used a four-speed gearbox, and had a top speed of 85 mph.

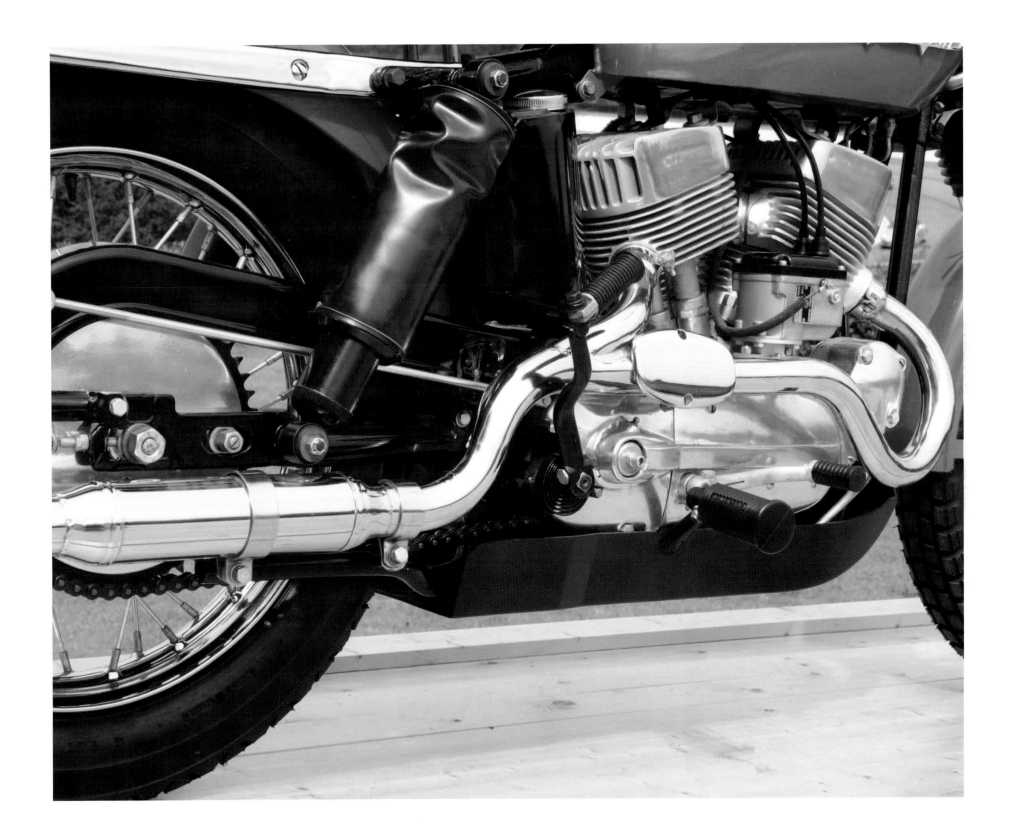

By 1934, class A racing was becoming too expensive for many and with the Depression hitting hard, a new class was introduced. Class C racing was aimed at the lower end of the market and involved everyday machines such as the Harley-Davidson WLDR, which was fully equipped for the road and able to be ridden to races – a stipulation of the rules.

For 1941 the WR was available to riders – private and factory – and carried Harley-Davidson hopes for the next decade. The WRTT came later and could be raced as a flat track or road racer, each having its own specification as far as brakes, wheels, and weight allowances were concerned.

The flathead KR models were the backbone of American dirt track racing from 1952 to 1969. Because these machines were constantly 'tweeked' by both tuners and riders, no two machines are the same.

The 45 cubic inch, air-cooled, side-valve, V-Twin could pump out nearly 50 hp, and could give the British vertical twins, a good run for their money.

On a slippery surface, a skilled rider could turn the uneven power delivery to his advantage. Telescopic front forks were fitted at the front but the rear remained rigid.

Once again racing came to a grinding halt as the Second World War enveloped the world. It would be 1948 before racing was to be resumed and now the Europeans had started infiltrating the United States with their machines. The model to come out of Harley-Davidson at this time was the KR, which was a development of the Model K. Initial production was slow but by 1955 there were five models available: KHK super sport solo, KHRM, KR dirt tracker, KRTT (probably the most successful Harley-Davidson racer ever), and the KHRTT.

The simple and easy-to-read instrumentation of the XR-TT, ridden by Pasolini.

Renzo Pasolini was born in the Adriatic seaside resort of Rimini, Italy. He loved motocross but went onto road racing with Aermacchi and Benelli motorcycles. He was tragically killed in an accident with Jarno Saarinen at Monza, Italy, in 1973.

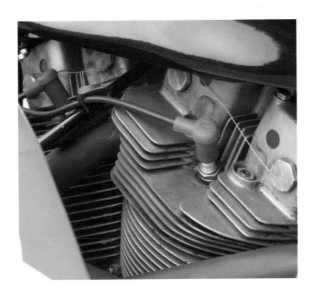

This is the XR-TT machine Pasolini raced in 1972. The engine was an air-cooled Harley-Davidson, 45 cubic inch (750cc) unit, which produced 90 hp and had a top speed in excess of 160 mph.

Although more at home on 250cc and 350cc machines, Pasolini also raced the 750cc machine in Ontario, Canada, where he finished a very respectable third overall.

The XLR-TT was Harley-Davidson's production racer, designed to compete in scrambles or 'TT' events, where the engine capacity was limited to 900cc.

More names came to the fore: Paul Goldsmith took the KRTT to a win at Daytona in 1953, Joe Leonard won eight of the eighteen Grand National races in 1954, on his Tom Sifton-tuned Harley-Davidson, and Brad Andres is well known for his three wins in the Daytona 200. For 1957, Dick O'Brien was made race manager at Harley-Davidson, and for 1958 Carroll Resweber became the first man to win four consecutive Grand National Motorcycle Championships, all on Harley-Davidson machines.

At the beginning of the 1960s Harley-Davidson bought out the ailing Aermacchi motorcycle business at Varese in Italy. With legendary riders such as Renzo Pasolini and Kel Carruthers racing these machines, some great successes were attained, even against the likes of Giacomo Agostini and Mike Hailwood, on their multi-cylinder MV machines. From the original Sprint of 1961 sprang all manner of racing machines. A competition scrambler and the CRS attained some good results in the hands of Bart Markel and Fred Nix. A road racing version of the CRS became the CRTT, and in 1968 the Sprint engine was increased to 350cc, with the scrambler being redesignated ERS.

The main competition at this time was the triumph 650cc TT Special, and the XLR was a good match for it. The engine internals were pure racing components.

Although the engine appeared to be similar to the production model, it had a shorter stroke and larger bore, giving it a higher rpm, which produced more power, whilst keeping the capacity the same.

The XLR had telescopic front forks and twin rear shock absorbers. Brakes were drum both at the front and rear. Top speed was 115 mph.

The mid-1960s also saw the British giving the Americans a good run for their money in the bigger engine sizes, not a situation appreciated back home in the United States. Triumphs and BSA/Matchless were stealing the show, although Reiman and Bart Markel did manage some good results, as did Cal Rayborn at Daytona in 1969, and Mert Lanwill took the overall championship in the same year.

The Ala D'Oro Aermacchi was a development of the Bianchi designed Chimera. It was basically stripped of its bodywork and fitted with a larger engine. This machine was then modified and made available as a 250cc racer for private entrants. When Harley-Davidson took on the Aermacchi concern, this was an ideal machine for them to make available to the current crop of racers.

The Aermacchi 350 Ala D'Oro was originally conceived as a scrambles machine, but was later dropped to accommodate road racing activities. Renzo Pasolini and Gilberto Milani, acted as works rider-testers, developing the machine through the next few years.

The 350 Ala D'Oro was known as the CRTT in the United States. Pasolini managed a very unexpected third place in the 1968 World Championships.

Well ventilated front drum brakes were needed for the 350, which was giving the pack of multi-cylinder adversaries a good run for their money.

1980 XR-750

Produced in 1971, the XR evolved from a heavy, iron head and barreled machine, which could barely produce 60 hp, to becoming a totally dominant machine in class 'C' dirt racing, with an output close to 100hp. The change came with the new, all-alloy engine, introduced in 1972. This particular machine was built in 1980 from the original specifications. It is fitted with twin Mikuni carburettors, front Marzocchi telescopic forks, has no brakes and a top speed of 125mph.

It was quite obvious that at the beginning of the 1970s, Harley-Davidson needed a new big racing machine. This came in 1971 in the form of the XR-750. Unfortunately it was not an instant success, but when the machine was relaunched in 1972, with a new lighter alloy engine designed by Pieter Zylstra, it took the same designation but was now known as the 'alloy XR.' The new machine was a completely different animal and went on to dominate American flat track racing, as well as achieving several other honours, such as the Transatlantic races in the hands of Cal Rayborn. Even taking these victories into account, the early 1970s were not a good time for the Harley-Davidson company, both on the track and off.

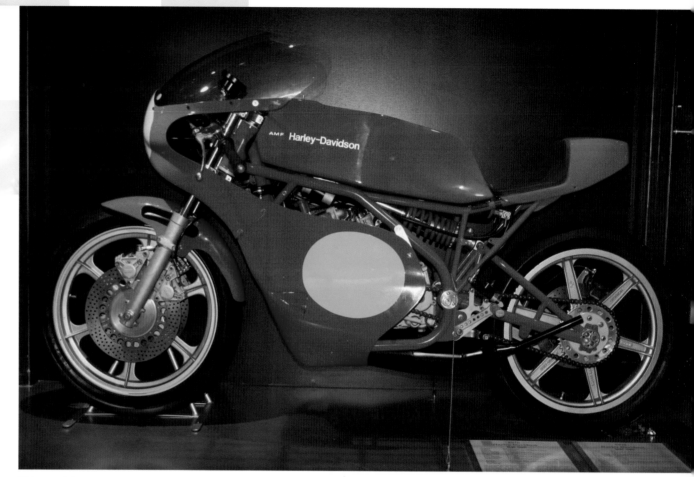

This machine was originally built by Harley-Davidson's Italian subsidiary, Aermacchi, for the 1975 race season, but lack of development left it uncompetitive.

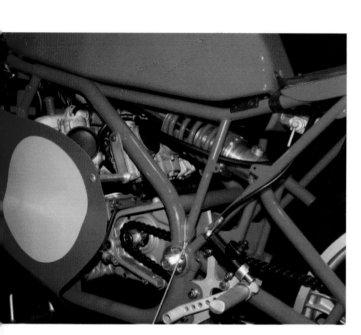

To improve the chassis performance, Aermacchi turned to well-known, Italian, specialist chassis builders, Bimota. They constructed four machines, of which this is one. The engine is a water-cooled, twin-cylinder, two-stroke unit of 488cc. There are four Dell'Orto carburettors, two per cylinder, and a special front brake design.

The Aermacchi connection continued to play a part in the Harley-Davidson racing scene through to the mid-1970s, the machines now wearing the AMF/Harley-Davidson badge, the company having been taken over by AMF. The team was led by the legendary Walter Villa, who seemed to make these machines work, even though they lacked a little potential. He took the Italian GP in this same year and went on to win the 250cc World Championship in 1974, 1975, and 1976, when he also took the 350cc title.

Other Aermacchi-based machines to be seen in the mid-1970s were the RR250cc of 1972, the Sprint SX 350cc in 1973, and the Z-90 of 1975. With the onslaught from Japan though, it was becoming increasingly difficult to match what was coming from the likes of Honda and Kawasaki, and finally the Aermacchi concern, now in financial trouble too, was sold to another Italian company, Cagiva.

It was by now obvious that the Aermacchi side of the business was not doing very well. Many machines had come and gone and sales had been good, but by the mid 1970s, all that was in the past. Several more machines were produced in the 125cc to 350cc range; this is the 1975 Aletta Corsa 125cc racing machine. It wasn't long after this that Aermacchi was finally closed down.

In the United States, things seemed to be going from bad to worse although the legendary Jay Springsteen held the American flag high with his domination of the dirt oval racing scene. It was in the early 1980s that the new BOTT (Battle of The Twins) race series started, allowing Harley-Davidson to regain its composure. The first event took place at Daytona in 1981, the engine size was limited to 1000cc, and the series was made up of eight races. The first year was somewhat experimental for the Harley team, but after 1982 they took it a little more seriously and entered the Dick O'Brien machine named 'Lucifer's Hammer,' a bike that would go down in the history books. Ridden by Springsteen, it won the 1983 race in style and went on to win the BOTT series GP title between 1984 through 1986, ridden also by Gene Church.

Not much in the way of instrumentation, but then who needs it on a race machine.

No doubting who rides this machine. Jay Springsteen still enjoys being out there on the tarmac mixing it with the best, and this is the machine he uses.

Owner Keith Campbell, is happy to leave his beautiful XRTT in the capable hands of Joe Brown to build, and the engine is tuned by Carl Patrick in Ohio, who is considered to be the world's best XR tuner - bar none.

Seen here is Gene Church on his Harley-Davidson XR750, during the Battle of the Twins road race, at the Daytona 200.

In 1998 Harley announced their own race series for the 883 Sportster, the inaugural race being won by a British rider Nigel Gale. Harley had also decided to enter its VR1000 in the AMA Superbike series, their first race taking place at Daytona in 1994. The rider was Miguel du Hamel and it wasn't a great start. Between breakdowns and lack of power, the machine performed badly. Many tried to improve the performance and reliability but without much luck, even though it did become competitive for a short spell. Harley persevered at the BOTT F1 races with 'Daytona Weapon,' a Takehiko Shibazaki design, and in 1997 with 'Golden Balls,' ridden by Springsteen, and then in 1998 with 'Weapon 2,' complete with British designed frame. It seems the days of the Wrecking Crew are never to be repeated. A period in Harley-Davidson history that will forever be cherished and never forgotten, with so many of its riders going on to take their place in the American Motorcycle Hall of Fame.

In action here is Scott Parker, whose career achievements included: nine-time AMA Grand National Champion, all-time record 94 Grand National Championship race wins, including 55 AMA National Mile wins, 35 AMA Half-Mile wins, and three-time winner of AMA Pro Athlete of the Year.

Harley-Davidson Alphabet

Designations, and in particular the Harley-Davidson series, can be confusing. Shown here is a simplified explanation of what some of the designations generally relate to, although even these are not always one hundred percent complete.

DYNA Glide

FX:	Superglide, Kick start
FXB:	Sturgis Belt (80,81 and 82ci)
FXD:	Dyna Super Glide
FXDB:	Dyna Sturgis (1991)
FXDC:	Dyna Super Glide Custom
FXDG:	Dyna Glide/Sturgis
FXDL:	Dyna Low Rider
FXDS-CON:	Dyna Convertible
FXDWG:	Dyna Wide Glide
FXDX:	Dyna Super Glide Sport
FXDXT:	Super Glide T-Sport
FXE:	Superglide Electric Start
FXEF:	Fatbob
FXLR:	FX Lower Rider/Evolution
FXR:	Rubber Mount Super Glide
FXRDG	Disc Glide
FXRP	Police or pursuit - Defender
FXRS:	FXR Sport
FXRS-CON:	FXR Sport Convertible
FXRS-SP:	Low Rider Sport Edition
FXRT:	FXR Touring
FXS:	Low Rider/Shovelhead
FXSB:	Low Rider Belt

Softail

FXST:	Softail Standard
FXSTB:	Night Train
FXSTBI:	Night Train EFI
FXSTC:	Softail Custom
FXSTD:	Softail Deuce
FXSTS:	Springer Softail
FXWG:	Wide Glide
FLST:	Heritage Softail
FLSTC:	Heritage Classic

FLSTF:	Fat Boy
FLSTFI:	15th anniversary Fat Boy
FLSTN:	Nostalgia and 2005 Softail Deluxe
FLSTS:	Heritage Springer
FLSTSC:	Springer Softail Classic

Touring

FL:	Four-Speed Dresser
FLH:	Four-Speed Electra Glide
FLHS:	FLT with windshield and less goodies S = Sport
FLHPI:	Road King police model
FLHR:	Road King
FLHRCI:	Road King Classic
FLHS:	Electra Glide Sport
FLHT:	Electra Glide Standard
FLHTC:	Electra Glide Classic
FLHTCSE:	Screamin Eagle Electra Glide
FLHTPI:	Electra glide police model
FLHTCUI:	Ultra Classic Electra Glide
FLT:	Rubber Mount Dresser
FLTC:	Rubber Mount Dresser Classic
FLTCU:	Rubber Mount Dresser Classic Ultra
FLTR:	Road Glide

FLTRI:	Road Glide EFI
FLTRSEI:	Screamin Eagle Road Glide

VRSC:	(V-TWIN Racing Street Custom)
VRSCA:	1st model of the V-ROD family
VRSCB:	Same as VRSCA except: Adjustable tubular handlebars, minimalist instrumentation, black painted frame, calipers, hand controls, shock springs and engine highlights
VRSCD:	Night Rod
VRSCR:	Roadster-inspired street rod

Sportsters:

XL:	Sportster 883
XL883:	Sportster Hugger
XL883C:	Sportster 883 Custom
XL 883L:	Sportster (specifically for smaller riders)
XL883R:	Dirt track-inspired
XL1100:	Sportster 1100
XL1200:	Sportster 1200
XL1200C:	Sportster 1200 Custom
XL1200R:	1200 Roadster
XL1200S:	Sportster 1200 Sport
XLCH:	4-Speed Sportster, kick start
XLCR:	Cafe Racer 1000
XLH:	Sportster 883
XLH883:	Sportster 883 Hugger
XLH883R:	Sportster 883R
XLH1200:	1200
XLH1200S:	Sport
XLS:	Four-Speed Sportster Roadster
XLX:	Four-Speed 1000cc Ironhead
XR1000:	XLH with XLR Heads

X - Sportsters. These descend from the K series, 1952-56

XL- Series started in 1957. They are 'unit construction' (engine & transmission share a common case)

L - High compression (7.5:1 in 1957)

H - Starting in 1958 came the XLH, meaning Higher-power or High-compression (9:1) or Hot

C - Also in 1958 was the XLCH. The C was intended to mean 'Competition'

CR- Cafe racer style, with bikini fairing

LT- Touring, with bigger tank, thicker seat, and hard bags

The first letter of the model designator reveals the engine series:

First character:

G - Servi-car three wheeler, 1937 to 1972

E - Overhead valve 61 cubic inch 'big twin' (Engine/trans separated)

F - Overhead valve 74,80 or 88 cubic inch 'big twin'

FL - 80 to 88 cubic inches and a fat front tire. (Also 74' 1941-82)

K - Side valve 45 and 55 cubic inch sports bike that replaced the WL in 1953 and was replaced by the Sportster in 1957. It had many design features that were carried over to the Sportster

U - Side valve 74 or 80 cubic inch 'big twin'

V - Side valve 74 cubic inch 1930-36. (Also 1935-36 VLH, VHS 80)

W - Side valve 45 cubic inch made 1937 to 1952

X - Sports and special construction. Applied to 1918-1922 opposed twin Sport, 1944 military opposed twin, and 1957 to present Sportster

The second letter of the model designator reveals the Front end (except sportsters):

X - Narrow tire and sport forks

L - Wide front tire and Hydra-Glide front forks

(FX originally meant 'Factory Expirimantal' The first one was the Super Glide FX)

The third letter of the model designator reveals the frame style:

D - 'Dyna' frame (with the rubber mounted motor)

HT - 'Highway Touring' frame

ST - 'Softail' frame

The next letter(s) indicates the model bike within the frame family:

A - Military (Army) version (except GA, Servi-car without tow bar)

B - Battery start (early models), Belt drive (early 80's) Black paint. (1995-6 model, the Bad Boy)

C - Classic, Competition, Custom, various others meanings

D - Dyna, the newest frame and engine mount design

DG - Disc Glide

E - Electric start

F - Foot shift (when the standard was hand-shift) and now 'Fat Boy'

H - varied between High performance, hand shift and Heavy duty

I - Signifies Fuel Injection

L - Big fat front tire

LR- Low Rider (though many Low Riders don't include LR in the model ID)

N - Nostalgia

P - Police version

R - Rubber mounted engine (some models) racing version (other models)

ST- Soft Tail

S - Springer

S - (without following T) Sports version

T - Touring

WG - Wide Glide

X - Sportster or sportster-type front end and Skinny front tire

Reproduced by kind permission:
www.factoryfat.com

Index

Acknowledgments

Putting a book together with the opportunity of shooting most, or all new pictures, doesn't come along very often. So when I was asked to put together this particular book, I made it my business to see if I could find a new source of Harley-Davidson pictures.

I soon came to the conclusion that the only way I was going to do that, and still stay in my budget, was to do it myself. So I put my photographer's hat on, made some phone calls and followed up some leads - and what leads they turned out to be. It is these people and organisations that I would like to thank; people who put themselves out to accommodate me and help me to feature some of the rarest and most interesting Harley-Davidson motorcycles on the planet:

Barbers Vintage Motorsport Museum, Birmingham, Alabama, USA.

I would like to thank Brian Slark for making my shoot a possibility, and for the other leads he gave me - the Mexican meal was great too!

I would like to thank Ken and Joe for doing all the donkey work, although I got the impression that they quite enjoyed re-arranging the exhibits too - thanks guys.

I would also like to thank Mr Barber for allowing me to disrupt the daily routine of his incredible museum.

Wheels Through Time Museum, Maggie Valley, North Carolina, USA.

There is no way of expressing just what joy I got from being at this museum. Dale Walksler describes it as a working museum, and he is right on the button with that! The exhibits themselves are a treasure, and there is enough memorabilia there to keep you occupied for several days. As for the actual motorcycles, well they are just breathtaking. Don't even bother to ask if any of them work, they do, and Dale takes no greater delight than to demonstrate them for you - restored or not! Be it the earliest Silent Grey fellow, a knucklehead or a panhead, they all come out of the shed, with a noise that will send a shiver of excitement right down to your socks.

Dale, Matt, Steve Banks (Public Relations Manager), and all the rest of your wonderful staff, I want to say a HUGE thanks, and without fail I will be back.

Keith Campbell and Joe Brown - How can I not tell everybody that I slept in the same bed that Springer Springsteen and many other stars have - in the best 'shed' I ever stayed in! Thank you both so much - great home cooking, not sure about the grits!

American Classic Motorcycle Co., Asheboro, North Carolina, USA - I will always remember that dodgy lift. Thank you so much for getting out, and allowing me to shoot, all those special machines you have.

A BIG thanks must also go to the following for their contribution and/or help:

Robert and Charlotte Brunner.
Harley-Davidson UK
Stratstone Harley-Davidson, Wolverhampton, West Midlands, UK.
Birmingham Harley-Davidson, West Midlands, UK.
P122 - 125 Courtesy of the Andrew Morland Photo Library, UK.
P155 Courtesy of the Don Morley Photo Library, UK.

All the kind people whose names I never got, who allowed me to shoot their machines.